PORTSMOUTH

'The Good Old Days'

PORTSMOUTH
'The Good Old Days'

THE VICTORIAN & EDWARDIAN CITY RECALLED BY RICHARD ESMOND
COMPILED AND ILLUSTRATED BY ANTHONY TRIGGS

HALSGROVE

First published in 2002 by Halsgrove
Copyright © 2002 Anthony Triggs

ISBN 1 84114 219 0

British Library Cataloguing-in-Publication-Data
A CIP data for this book is available from the British Library

HALSGROVE
Halsgrove House
Lower Moor Way
Tiverton EX16 6SS
T: 01884 243242
F: 01884 243325
www.halsgrove.com

Printed and bound in Great Britain by Bookcraft, Midsomer Norton

CONTENTS

ACKNOWLEDGEMENTS

As always I must thank my publisher, Steven Pugsley, for his advice and encouragement, and so many other friends who have come forward to help, including Alf Harris, Ron Brown, Peter Rogers, Andrew Perrin, Tom Dethridge, Roy Adams and Bob Irwin of J.A. Hewes, photographers. Two other people deserve special thanks: Elizabeth Hughes, Richard Esmond's granddaughter, for her support, and of course my wife Sue, whose help and encouragement is always there without fail.

FOREWORD

tudents of local history will no doubt know two small blue-covered paperbacks, *The Charm of Old Portsmouth* and *Portsmouth Not So Old.* These two slim volumes were written and illustrated by Portsmouth-born author Richard Esmond, and were published by Gale & Polden when that company had its little shop on the corner of Stanhope Road and Edinburgh Road in Portsmouth.

Both books sold out very swiftly and today are sought-after items among collectors of Portsmouth's history.

Esmond's writings, with his delicate pen drawings, were also regular features of the then *Portsmouth Evening News,* and over the years he gathered a following of loyal readers. His last series of articles told the story of his early life and the Portsea street in which he was born.

Richard Esmond was born Frederick Thomas Triggs in a tiny house in Orange Street in the January of Queen Victoria's Jubilee Year of 1887, and was the younger brother of my grandfather, William Richard Triggs. He adopted his nom de plume from the Christian name of his father, Richard Triggs, and from the maiden name of his mother, Mary Anne Esmond.

He went into the teaching profession and moved away from the area, but could never forget his love of the city of his birth, and eventually returned and settled in Southsea upon his retirement in 1947.

He was a kind and gentle man, and was proud of the fact that he had served three sovereigns – Edward VII in the 4th Volunteer Battalion of the Oxfordshire and Buckinghamshire Light Infantry; George V in the First World War in the Hampshire Fortress Royal Engineers (Territorials), later being commissioned in the Army Service Corps; and HM Queen Elizabeth II when he enlisted in the RNVR at the age of seventy-one – possibly the oldest man so to do.

He died in August 1967 at the age of eighty, just weeks after his last series of articles was published.

His recollections of childhood and his observations of the changes in the city upon his return make fascinating reading and, with 250 nostalgic illustrations, give an insight into the Portsmouth of the past, described by a former headmaster who cared deeply about the city he loved.

This new book *Portsmouth – 'The Good Old Days'* will, I hope, preserve for the future the skills of a true man of Portsmouth.

Anthony Triggs, Portchester 2002.

The pace of life was so much slower in late-Victorian and early-Edwardian days, as this image of Clarence Parade, Southsea, so eloquently shows.

A lone motorist has plenty of room to negotiate the junction of Palmerston Road and Osborne Road at Handleys' Corner.

Cyclists wait at the traffic lights on the corner of Elm Grove and Grove Road South on what is obviously a warm summer's day.

The flags are out in this 1905 picture of Osborne Road at a time when large hats and parasols were all the rage. The decorations were in honour of the visit to Portsmouth of the French fleet.

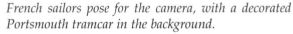

French sailors pose for the camera, with a decorated Portsmouth tramcar in the background.

INTRODUCTION

Public houses are not the only places where questions of the day, national and local, are argued out and settled; or if not settled, at least aired.

The shelters along Southsea front, even in the winter season, often see the thrashing out of burning questions by men (and women) for most of whom working days are obviously over. It was a sort of Parade Parliament – and why not? Opportunities for social and sociable contact are few enough, especially for older people.

One subject which crops up continually, a hardy perennial, is 'the good old days – or were they?'

'These days are not like the old days,' some say, and the cynic comments: 'They never were!'

I have heard at various times in these shelter meetings most of the arguments on the subject, with many others, too.

One relates how sixpence used to buy an ounce of baccy, a pint of beer, and a dozen boxes of matches. Another scornfully compares today's meat ration with a 'good tuck in' in the poorest house in bygone days, of bacon, cabbage, and suet pudding all boiled together in one pot!

Yet another describes how in a little local public house the dustmen with their horses and carts on the way to the dump used to call for a top of cottage loaf, a piece of cheese nearly as big, and half a pint of beer. The bill was threepence. Lunch and drink for a hungry man. But wait! In cold weather the beer had to be heated, and a bit of root ginger added – and there were growls if the taproom fire was not roaring up the chimney! And often a pickled onion or two were thrown in to liven up the bread and cheese.

These and many other wistful pictures of the economic past have come up. After one such session I was left alone in a shelter and began to muse about what it really is that the old people mourn about the 'good old days.' Much of what I heard is just a matter of change in money values.

But thought was interrupted by a group of the bonny babies of today passing along, and there was one way, thought I, in which the new days beat the old days hollow.

Gone are the rickety legs and the pale stringy babies so often seen years ago. Gone are those once-familiar and horrible funeral carriages with a sort of box under the driver's seat for a baby's coffin.

This was an interruption, and I began again to wonder. Was it really what sixpence would buy years ago, or how much one could get to eat cheaply that older people look back on with longing eyes?

Did that sort of thing constitute 'the good old days'?

At this point I became dreamingly aware that an old familiar sound was thrusting itself into my attention, and that I had not for many years let that sound weave itself into my thoughts. It was what Matthew Arnold called 'the grating roar of pebbles on the beach.' I realise that now I never heard it as I used to – with an easy receptive mind. It was a sound tied up with days of youth, with lying on the beach in summer heat after a bathe, eyes drowsily closed and thoughts a-wander against the background of that rhythmic surge.

It may sound strange but I thought then that I began to see just why the good old days were good. It was little or nothing to do with prices or food. It was because, in those times before 1914, one did listen to such sounds in nature, hear them and get acquainted with them.

But that is only one small aspect of what I mean. Now in the raucous roar of modern life, its worries, public and private, its wars and rumours of wars, there is no time for tasting the simple and lovely things with a free and unhurried mind. No wonder things are not what they were, for the world has twice been dumped into a sack, taken for a ride, shaken up and tipped out breathless and bruised.

A boy or girl in the old days could plan a career, plot out his or her life, and barring 'Acts of God' could rely on a reasonable chance of it coming out as planned.

I think it is, more than anything, that loss of calm and orderly living that older people miss most, whether they realise it or not.

The cynic who says the times never were what they were is off the mark, for it may be that there has never before been such a great break in the conditions of life in the space of one ordinary lifetime.

So let those whose lives have covered that period of change have their say. It may be that the old days were better, but for more intangible reasons than beer, baccy and food. Man shall not live by bread alone, and perhaps mankind has lost some of the other things that matter most.

Richard Esmond April 10 1951

The North Pole was Under the Harbour Station

(First published 12 October 1950)

What is it that makes so strong and affectionate the ties between this city of Portsmouth and its people? Writers and poets, ancient and modern, have remarked on love of country, but this affection for one's native town, a more localised love, seems sometimes even stronger.

Born and brought up in Portsmouth, I recently returned to live here after thirty years' absence. More leisure makes possible the revisiting of places so well remembered, in and around the city, and inevitably memories of fifty and sixty years ago come crowding in.

The first haunt of boyhood I visited was the Common Hard. On the way I dug right into old Portsea and looked for Bonfire Corner, but could scarcely find it. There where I first went to school in 1890 and where in a greengrocer's shop lived a childhood friend named John Cobb, it was difficult to place old landmarks.

The school is gone – swallowed up in a brewery. Daniel Street, where we got the home-made bulls-eyes at 2oz for a ha'penny, is gone too. And sedate Marlborough Row? What a different place was Portsea then! There seems to have been wholesale migration, Portsea to Portchester, Fratton to Farlington, reversing the ancient trend. I followed round the old Queen Anne brick wall of the dockyard towards the Hard. Here was not so much change, but coming out of the end of Queen Street showed that the block of old houses making up Camden Alley had been cleared away.

There is a spot on the pavement under the dockyard wall near the end of Queen Street that I shall never forget. Drunkenness in those days was certainly more common than now. On that pavement I saw as a child, a terribly drunken naval stoker fighting against two or three of those big raw-boned men we used to call water police. He was on the ground and still resisting when another water policeman rushed at the double into the fray and jumped with both feet on to the man's stomach, and so ended the disturbance.

At the main gate, the familiar old brickwork made a new appeal to my older eyes, but I missed the little hole in the wall where the dockies lit their pipes on leaving, matches being forbidden in the dockyard.

But here was the Hard at last, suffering from bomb damage and showing many gaps, and certainly not so many pubs as there were fifty years ago. And where were 'the logs?' I could feel again the August sun of half a century and more ago on my back, as we lay flat on our bellies on those logs, noses touching water, holding a few yards of string at the end of which was a cod's head begged from a fishmonger. At the bottom of six or eight feet of quiet water we watched the crabs approach and cling to the bait. Then the gradual pulling up of the line, inch-by-inch, with crab on the cod's head, and one's mate with cap cupped in hand ready to grab the crab when it broke water. Often the crab dropped off, but the cap invariably caught plenty of water at least, and some not-so-fresh cod's heads. We used to boil and eat those small crabs and enjoy them.

Are there any Common Hard kingers now? The lawless young rascals who haunted that place in those days were so called. They cared for nobody, and the police were more or less helpless to deal with them, for when chased they would retire to their own dark corners among the piles and mud under the Harbour Station, probably to resume their 'pitch and toss' with the coppers gained at low tide, thrown down into the mud from the railings by passers by. The sight of the near-naked bodies black with harbour mud from head to foot shocked some people and amused others. At least the lucky finder of the coin among the many youngsters delving for it in the liquid mud always tipped a black face upwards at the donor to thank him.

There was a far away place under there known as the North Pole, which we ordinary boys never explored.

On past the station steps and down to the pontoon, where we spent many hazardous hours of boyhood, of which our mothers did not know, fortunately for their peace of mind. Behind the pontoon there used to be a group of wherries, mostly owned by one Lampard. I wonder if those wherries were a hangover from the days when rowing boats were the only means of crossing the harbour. I suppose they finally disappeared when the *Victory* was taken into the dockyard and visitors to her no longer needed boats.

The pontoon cannot be quite the same now, for in the left-hand corner, we used to be able, by leaning over at the risk of overbalancing, to see round the corner of the Railway Pier to the Camber mouth. I remember so looking once to see a ship sunk off the Camber with only one funnel and masts showing above the water. Was it the *Dandy Dinmont*?

There too, we used to love to stand and watch the water churned up by the paddles of the departing Ryde boats. 'Ginger beer,' we used to say, and feel thirsty.

Another vivid memory was of a great white ship with her bows rammed into the railway viaduct, which ran from the station to the dockyard. I believe it was the *Crocodile*, one of the old Indian troopers.

Two grand sights are missing now. Where is the old *St Vincent* that made so many tough and efficient sailormen of the old sort? And what a gap there is over there by Gosport Hard, where the *Victory* would lay for so long that she seemed an unalterable part of the harbour scene.

One thing about the pontoon struck me as quite unaltered – the ferry boats. Are they the same old *Venus* and *Ferry Princess*? If the same, how long have some of them been working, and how many times have they cleverly dodged the harbour tides?

New to me were the rails that separate comers and goers. Convenient perhaps, and safer, in these hurrying days with a growing Gosport, but somehow they take from the pontoon as a free and easy lookout over the fascinating life of the harbour.

My trip to the Hard and back was comfortably done for a few pence on the city trolley buses. What a change from the days of A.W. White's horse buses and horse tramcars.

The long line of buildings face out on to the Hard in the days of horse trams. Some of the logs from which Richard Esmond and his friends fished are visible on the right of the picture.

The mudlarks delved into the ooze to search for coins thrown by passengers making their way to and from the railway station and the Gosport ferries.

The main gate of the dockyard was, and still is, an important facet of the Hard at Portsea.

Many old-time sailors learned their trade aboard the old wooden wall HMS St Vincent, *moored off Gosport.*

Another ship to bear the historic name of St Vincent *was launched in Portsmouth in 1908. She was a battleship of the Bellerophon class, and at that time was the largest warship to be built in Portsmouth.*

This postcard shows Portsmouth harbour station, beneath which the Portsea youngsters had an area known as the North Pole. A train can be seen on the railway viaduct into the dockyard.

Bonfire Corner recorded by the camera in the quieter days just after the war.

One of the earliest ferries to ply between Portsmouth and Gosport was the Frances, seen here pulling in to the pontoon at Gosport. The Frances was one of the first vessels of the Gosport and Portsea watermen's Steam Launch Company, and began service in 1878.

Would-be passengers await the arrival of the ferry from Gosport in the days when all men wore hats and every woman carried a parasol.

When They Called it the Town Hall Square

(First published 14 December 1950)

A dark wet evening, asphalt shining in the light of tall arc lamps, the clip-clop of a passing hansom cab, and hurdy-gurdy on a stick played by a bent and bearded old man, with the great bulk of the Town Hall looming over all, its lighted clock face in the clouds – that is my first memory of Portsmouth's centre.

Back in the 1890s, Portsmouth was more compact than now and the square was more definitely the heart of the town. Asphalt and arc lamps were comparatively new things and most of the roads were still plain macadam. The lamplighter with his long pole was still a familiar sight.

The Town Hall itself was able to accommodate police headquarters, the central library, the education department and Treasurer's offices and much else, as well as the council chambers. In the great hall on Saturday evenings used to be held the penny popular concerts run by the municipality. For tuppence one could be superior and look down on the groundlings from the balcony. The concerts were mainly vocal, varied by well-known local players at the great organ, but the biggest crowds were always drawn by the old minstrel shows.

Occasionally the big hall was the scene of an important political meeting. At one of these, during a general election, Sir Henry Campbell-Bannerman was to speak. I remember nothing of the speeches I heard, but I do recall waiting in the dense crowd on or around the semi-circular steps on the north side before the door opened.

These were pre-queue days, and when the doors did open the tightly-packed crowd carried me up the steps without effort on my part. There was a technique for surviving in those crowds – bend the forearms up in front of the chest, have no corns, and leave your watch at home.

It may have been in connection with the same political campaign that I remember watching in the crowd the general election results cast on a screen outside the *Evening News* offices in Stanhope Road. There was much noisy enthusiasm on both sides. Later we went to await the local result in the square packed with thousands waiting for either a blue or red flare high up in the dome.

On that windy south-eastern corner of the Town Hall opposite the gas company offices, I remember coming into contact with a hero, and that literally. For, with head down against the wind, I bumped into a broad-shouldered figure coming from the direction of the dockyard. He apologised charmingly, for my fault, and went on. That fine man rests now in a spot much more bleak than that corner, for he was Shackleton of the Antarctic.

Over the way it used to be a fine sight in the old days to see the horse-drawn fire engine dash out of the stables at a gallop on the way to a fire. It was so much more thrilling than in these mechanised days to see those lovely horses clattering along at full pelt with the heavy engine and the shining brass helmets and clanging bell behind. They got there by sheer enthusiastic muscular power as though they understood perfectly the need for such urgent haste. They were worth a visit too, as they stood ready harnessed in the stable before a call, every bit of gear polished to the last rub and their coats shining like that of a wet seal.

Going back a bit, I remember the arrival home of the naval brigade from Ladysmith. We stood by the railings under the railway bridge and watched the men, bronzed by the African sun, march out of the town station. To us boys they were wonderful: of the company of those who came home from beating the Armada or from Trafalgar. Still farther back, to the first year or two of the 1890s, another memory comes from the entrance of Victoria Park under the railway arch. No war memorial stood there then, of course. Looking across the park on the inner curve of the wall by the arch there used to be a wooden bench. Walking one day through the arch into the park with my father, I was interested in a group of old men sitting on the bench in the sun. They wore medals on their jackets, and in answer to my question, my father said they were Crimean veterans. On a Sunday evening some years later I saw the newsboys dash out of the *Evening News* offices with a special edition giving the news of the Battle of Omdurman and the charge of the 21st Lancers. The boys were in such a galloping haste that people were snatching at their copies without any hope of getting change. It is difficult now in these war-soaked days to realise how important that small battle seemed. But it was welcomed as some satisfaction – long deferred – following the tragedy of General Gordon.

Restoration of the drill hall in Stanhope Road reminds me of a visit by Lord Roberts after the South African war. 'Bobs' was there with his small goatee, another of our great little men who was immensely popular with the Army.

Having come so far into Commercial Road a seasonable thought comes of Christmasses past, when the Landport Drapery Bazaar on the corner of Arundel Street, and the shops in the Arcade were the mecca of thousands of youngsters whose noses were pressed against the toy windows in delight and longing.

There was also Christmas shopping at Pinks on the corner of Surrey Street, where we went on the only alcoholic binge of the year by taking home (own bottle) a quart of drinkable Tarragona port for one shilling! Shall I call down the wrath of connoisseurs if I put childhood's little Christmas glass of port (akin to Bob Cratchitt's modest Christmas punch) in the same paragraph? Who shall measure these values?

The Town Hall Square was always a popular gathering place, never more so than in November 1918 when the mayor addressed this huge crowd to announce the armistice.

The Town Hall pillars form a dramatic background to the Easter Monday choral festival in 1910.

Queen Victoria would certainly not have been amused at this undignified removal in 1972 when work commenced on the redesigning of the Guildhall Square (as the Town Hall Square was renamed after Portsmouth became a city in 1926). After cleaning, the statue was brought back to its present position.

The Queen originally surveyed her domain from her plinth in the corner of the square.

Victoria Park seen in late-Victorian days when meeting to listen to the music in the small bandstand was evidently a popular pastime.

Guildhall Square begins to take on a new identity in 1975 as the construction of the huge civic office complex takes shape.

The square played host to many royal events including the Royal Family's return from South Africa in 1947.

A snowy between-the-wars scene at the entrance to Victoria Park near the railway arch.

The Connaught Drill Hall in Stanhope Road was rebuilt after the ravages of the Second World War.

The old Evening News *office in Stanhope Road where people used to gather to buy the first papers containing news of all the events, both national and international. Here the offices are decorated for the Silver Jubilee Review of the Fleet in 1935.*

Before Trees Graced the Common

(First published 22 January 1951)

What would Southsea be like without its common? Today, with its trees and splendid flower beds, its rock gardens, bowling greens, tennis courts and bandstand it is a very attractive place, but fifty years ago and more it was a treeless unplanned open space of rough grass and few paths. Long before Southsea grew up on its edge it was the haunt of footpads and the scene of many dark deeds.

My own earliest memory of the common dated from the very early 1890s. I was walking as a child with my father from the promenade at the eastern end of the castle across the common to the old battery. This used to lie under the castle wall east of the present castle café.

Naval reservists used the old battery for their drill. Its stout timbers inside suggested the old 'wooden walls' of England, and they were necessarily stout to carry the battery-mounted heavy guns of the old type looking out on the common through ports. The place even had the ship smell of rope yarn and tar.

A popular event on the common was the Queen Victoria birthday reviews of 24 May. The weather on those occasions seemed always to be perfect, sunny and hot – Queen's weather. The review was held on the stretch from Clarence Pier to where the naval memorial now stands. Most popular with us children used to be the naval contingent in their straw hats, hauling their field guns by long rope traces.

Their salute of 21 guns was the high spot of the review, and was often made more exciting by the antics of the startled mounts of the military officers, in their cocked hats and scarlet tunics. Then came the *feu de joie* by the military, which were drawn up in two very long ranks with rifles pointing into the air. They would fire their blanks, beginning at one end of the front rank and crackling along its whole length and down the rear rank, like boys running sticks along a railing.

The first avenue of the trees which so pleasantly break up the flat stretch of the common was I think that across the Ladies' Mile from the Queen's Hotel to the Lennox Mansions. It must be almost half a century old now and I remember that many Jeremiahs declared that the trees would never stand up to the wind, but considering their exposed position they are remarkably upright and free from a wind-swept lopsidedness. Those who now stroll in their shade on a hot day must bless the forethought of the town council of fifty years ago.

The Ladies' Mile and the castle gate seen from it brought back a memory of the common that still produces a chuckle. Where the skating rink now stands a party of pre 1914 Territorials at camp in the castle were doing company drill under a sergeant. I would not for the world cast any doubt on the efficiency of the sergeant or his squad, but many shouted orders and many and varied response from the men had resulted in something like chaos. When all were at least, and at last, still, and facing all ways, the sergeant, rifle on shoulder and a hopeless look in his eyes, pushed his cap up, scratched his head, and gave his last order, slowly and resignedly and not out of the drill book – 'Now sort yourselves out!'

A not so humorous memory of the common was of the evening when tens of thousands of people were on the seafront to see the fleet illuminations on the occasion, of the coronation of Edward VII. There was literally a cloudburst quite suddenly and in a matter of minutes all were soaked. Thousands ran splashing across the already flooded common, and I can say with no exaggeration at all that I was soaked to the skin.

On summer evenings the old concert parties, with a trolley for platform, would perform where the gardens now lie at the end of Burgoyne Road. Sometimes there was a party with a more ambitious sort of stage down in The Dell, and on the old South Parade Pier – fated to burn – the Musketeers would perform for threepence (reserved seat sixpence). Moonlight, no motor traffic or horns, and *Songs of Araby* or *The Bedouin's Love Song* could be heard across the common.

A well-known performer of those days was the Green Man who wore a mask while singing on his trolley on the common, and fluttered the hearts of young women because of his fine tenor rendering of the sentimental ballads of those days – and perhaps because of his mask.

A strange 'unknown' too used often to be heard in the dark on summer evenings along the parades, singing fine songs beautifully in a tenor voice. He sang apparently as the birds sing – for no reward – for at the near approach of anyone he would hasten away.

More in the region of fantasy than of memory was Spring-heeled Jack who was supposed to appear here and there like a will-o-the-wisp, either mounted on stilts or equipped with some wonderful spring apparatus in his boots for the purpose of tapping on the bedroom windows of the credulous.

Simpler days perhaps… But I think that this looking back of the older generation is not merely nostalgia for youthful days, but like the popular old-time dancing movement, a reaching back to times that really did have more savour, more graciousness, and less hurry.

In its early days the old semaphore station stood on Southsea Common, and was part of a chain of such buildings used to send messages from Portsmouth to London.

Deckchairs and parasols are all the fashion for a sunny day on the Ladies' Mile at Southsea.

Queen Victoria's birthday parades were popular attractions on the common. In 1898, because of heavy rain in the morning, the commanding officer countermanded the review orders and marched his troops back to barracks. However bluejackets of the naval brigade from HMS Excellent stood fast and did the entire review themselves. The sun came out as the standard was hoisted.

Much of the common was converted to leisure activities in the early part of the twentieth century. Games on the bowling greens and tennis courts proved a popular pastime.

Dancing around the bandstand was another popular pastime. After the war the bandstand was converted to a roller-skating rink, and today serves as a skateboard park.

The Dell at Southsea pictured in later days. It was here, as Richard Esmond recalls, that a temporary stage was set up to provide entertainment for Victorians.

A Portsdown Fair, Half a Century Ago

(First published 27 March 1951)

Steam organs and swing boats, boxing booths and gipsies, fat ladies and skeleton men, caravans and horses, streamers, ticklers and water squirts: a pandemonium of noises all the time; and in the evening a quickening of the whole tempo of the fair with naptha flares making a glow that was visible from Hilsea or Copnor – this was the Easter fair on Portsdown Hill in Victorian times.

Nowadays amusements have multiplied, and so-called fun fairs, outdoor and indoor are many. Not so then, which is perhaps why the old-fashioned fair, coming for a day or two and then away again, was such an exciting event. But not only for that reason, for the old-time fair still had about it something of the old Merrie England spirit.

What a sight it was years ago to see the crowds on Easter Monday making their way out of the town to Portsdown Hill. It was then really out of the town, for after Kingston Cross there were only scattered houses.

From North End junction onward the road was truly rural and dusty, bordered by fields with big elm trees. Where now is the shopping centre between Kingston Cross and North End, there was a real old country smithy – Boxall's –

although there was no 'spreading chestnut tree'.

Most of us youngsters on their way to the hill would stop at Boxall's for a look in, as youngsters have always done. For most would footslog to the fair, not having the cash for a ride to Cosham on the old horse trams. Many went in wagonettes or coster barrows with donkeys, and the narrow High Street at Cosham was rather like Epsom town on Derby morning.

But before reaching Cosham there was the long plod to Hilsea, and then on through the arches under the ramparts to the narrow iron swing bridge over Ports Creek. There was but one road through Cosham, of course; a definitely separate Cosham, with its own quiet charm on any other day but fair day.

From the London Road above the village a ramp on the left led up to a fairly level spot. Here was the end of the journey, and here was the fair in full swing. Youth can stomach noise, and there was plenty here. The cries of the stall-holders and boxing men, the yells from the swing boats and roundabouts, the enticement of the hoopla stalls and coconut shies were enough, but over-riding all was the peculiar pumping blast of the steam organs.

Underfoot the grass was trampled brown and flat and was littered with paper, orange peel and coconut shell. Always fascinating were the little figures on the organs that automatically beat triangles or blew trumpets. They jerkily moved head and arms and had something of a nightmarish quality about them.

Yells of laughter meant something like a donkey derby was taking place, as people hurriedly got out of the way to see the jockeys, usually sailors, gallop, trot or walk in any direction but the right on the backs of unwilling steeds. To ride facing the donkey's tail seemed to be considered correct.

There were boxing booths where dark brawny chaps stripped to the waist yelled their hardest from the platform in front of the gaily-painted booths, shouting a challenge to anyone to stand up to them for a given time for a money prize. And they always got contenders for the prize, but it was usually a thick ear.

Then you could have a go at a queer contraption like an enormous barometer standing up about 15 feet into the air. You had to hit mightily with a heavy mallet to make the indicator fly up and ring the bell at the top. It was fun to see the showmen, after so many failures by some hefty punter, swing the mallet with such a knack and deceptive ease and ring the bell every time.

There were always plenty of coconut shies. There was an ancient gipsy woman, coloured and wrinkled like a walnut, sitting with her crate of balls and smoking a black clay pipe not more than three inches long.

'Give us a draw gran,' shouted a sailor, winking at his mates.

'It'd make you sick, my son,' she said, and I suppose he smoked his pound of old navy plug every month.

Many were the booths of fat ladies and fortune tellers, and plenty of stalls offering oranges, nuts and apples. Barrows there were too, that held up great enticing glass bowls of yellow lemonade that simply created a thirst in a boy.

As the dusk fell, all the noise and fun were intensified. By then most of the youngsters had started back on the long trek home, probably chewing coconut often given them by open-handed sailors who liked the winning better than the eating, and couldn't carry an armful of coconuts anyway.

So homeward in the dark, with many glances back over the shoulder to the glow on the hill and the distant noise with the trumpet blare of the roundabout organs still audible.

And so to bed – and to sleep if undigested coconut permitted.

Many could not afford to ride the horse trams to the fair and had to make their way by foot to the slopes of Portsdown Hill.

Fairgoers would have passed through Kingston Cross at North End on their way to enjoy the pastimes on offer.

A single policeman supervises the junction at Gladys Avenue in the days when there was little in the way of traffic to control. The building in the centre, The Poplars, was demolished between the wars when the Southdown Bus Company offices were built.

The old smithy at North End was always a popular stopping point for youngsters on their way to the fair.

Cosham was a much quieter place in the early 1900s. Here a tram deposits passengers bound for the railway station.

The gallopers prove a big draw to visitors to the bank-holiday fair on the hill slopes. This evocative picture captured a jolly day out in late-Victorian days.

The long cavalcade of fairgoers would have passed through the ramparts at Hilsea. This picture shows workmen beginning to demolish the old brickwork prior to the construction of the new Portsbridge.

The fair continued until after the First World War, although by that time it was probably not as noisy as its Victorian counterpart.

A Portsdown and Horndean Light Railway tram makes its way to the station on the lower hill slopes as hundreds more people head towards the fair in this picture from the 1930s.

The circus often came to town. Here Bertram Mills's Circus has set up its show on the corner of Waite Street at Cosham, where the police station now stands.

The carrying of gas masks and tin helmets was a necessity at all times in the bleak wartime days, as shown by these fairgoers on their way to the hill slopes.

Old Milton Preferred a Quiet Life

(First published 2 July 1951)

Portsmouth, in the last couple of generations, has seeped all over the island of Portsea, and beyond, like liquid spilled on blotting paper.

In its spreading it has absorbed little places that once had their own separate existence and characteristics.

Milton is one such place, and far back it led the life of a typical English village. Its roads were narrow hedge-bound country roads, its church a village church. It had its gentry as its leading inhabitants, its village smithy in Priory Lane, its village school, and Portsmouth was a long country walk away.

There was one leading Milton family which almost was Milton – the Goldsmiths. Back in mid-Victorian days James Goldsmith owned much of the land and farmed it in the old style. The rule of this family hereabouts was probably the last example of feudalism that Portsea Island was to see. Feudalism did not always mean oppression, and with the kindly landlord it had its points. James Goldsmith was often seen in his top hat, and his dignified wife in bonnet and black silk dress of such stiffness that it would stand up of itself. She used to drive out of the gate opposite the old church in a low pony chaise of the sort that Queen Victoria drove. Inside the gate were the peacocks that the children used to stop to see and hear.

Their son was James Goldsmith the younger. There were many tales of young Master James, top-hatted and gaitered, which are still being told. He must have had a considerable share of public spirit and a vision of an expanding Portsmouth, for Milton Park, which used to be the immediate surroundings of his home, was his gift. He stipulated that all the fine trees were to be untouched – a splendid thought.

The family name is perpetuated in the name of the avenue that faces the park. A public house, which stood at the corner of Priory Lane in the avenue, was transferred as the Shepherd's Crook to the other side of the road to make a complete whole of the park.

There was a large house set well back from the road, with grounds stretching across the canal. In it lived, long ago, an Admiral Hallows in quiet country retirement full of good works. By the side of the house ran the quiet lane to the locks, which is now Locksway Road, and not so quiet as then.

On the main road opposite the Goldsmith residence was the little old church, although not old as village churches go. It was built in good imitation Norman style, with flint walls, like those of the vicarage, which still stands beside its site.

It was a church favoured for weddings by the romantically minded, and was sometimes known as the runaway church. It was never, however, a serious rival to Gretna Green! It had to give way to the bigger modern church when Milton began to grow. The churchyard still shows the tombs of the Goldsmith family and many of the families of old Milton.

There was a little village school of the old type where the big school now stands. The children went on outings to the tea gardens on Portsdown, conveyed tightly packed in Master James's farm wagons.

The smithy in Priory Lane was still at work within the memory of a great many people. Here the horses of the district were shod; iron tyres were made, heated, fitted to the wheels and shrunk tight by quick cooling with buckets of water.

In those old days the canal cut right through the village, with a bridge on the road by the White House, and another where Ironbridge Lane, off Locksway Road, still indicates its position.

The canal had a short inglorious working history. It was built with great enthusiasm and expectations to carry goods between Portsmouth and London by way of Arundel. It was opened in 1823, but within about a year Portsmouth people were complaining that the seawater in the canal contaminated their well water. There was not the piped supply then that we now enjoy. Business too was bad, and the canal just fell into disuse.

Its course from the locks at Langstone end to the White House is still quite plain. Only the frame of one of the lock gates remains.

From the White House the canal bed was what is now Goldsmith Avenue, filled in in 1896. It then went along to Fratton Bridge, and the course of the railway by Canal Walk follows it to a basin in Lower Arundel Street. One can peer over the front fences of many of the Goldsmith Avenue houses facing Milton Park and Fratton Park, and can still see the top of the bank of the old canal untouched. And the old cottage on the corner of Fratton Bridge, looking so strangely out of place, once looked down into the water of the canal. Such are some of the old wrinkles that peep out of the 'lifted' face of modern Portsmouth.

Milton today has a great deal to offer its residents. The park with its bowls and tennis, its trees, lawns and flower beds, the nearness to the sea both at Southsea and by the quiet shores of Langstone, the chances of sailing, boating and fishing, are not to be found everywhere. If the old village is a memory, the new Milton is not so bad.

The barn in Milton Park makes a picturesque scene in 1929.

Milton children often took trips to the tea gardens at the summit of Portsdown Hill.

One of the last pieces of old Milton shown at a time when modern development was overtaking history.

Milton Church seen on a quiet winter's day at the turn of the last century.

A favourite place to stop and take rest was the old canal locks at Milton, though even by the late 1880s, when this picture was taken, they were in a sad state of disrepair.

The old smithy at Milton was a favourite subject for early photographers.

Milton Creek with a group of old vessels moored along the foreshore.

Springtime in Milton in the quiet times before the Second World War changed everybody's lives.

Down Prospect Road to Scenes of Childhood

(First published 9 July 1951)

There is a bit of Portsmouth, which is full of interest but for the average dweller in the city is quite unknown and unvisited. Yet it runs almost within a stone's throw of busy Commercial Road, and attractive glimpses of it can be had down side streets from the top of a bus.

It is that stretch edging the harbour between the dockyard and Whale Island and known as Flathouse and Rudmore. This part of the city was much brighter than it is now and the quays and ships drew schoolboys from all around like a magnet.

On a fine day I went down to see how it compared with old times. I turned down Prospect Road and came out on Flathouse Quay. There were changes here for the main part of the quay is being extended. Also the view up the creek to the north corner of the dockyard is filled in by a huge floating dock. And quite close I recognised a familiar sight of old days; the old Royal Yacht *Victoria and Albert* with truncated masts and a sad look of shabby retirement.

The granite steps opposite Prospect Road, leading down to the deep water, took me back more than fifty years. I recalled small boys playing on those steps, and one of them had slipped off the side into the water and the other boys stood frozen with terror. There was a clatter of boots down the steps and a man's long arm stretched out and was just able to reach the drowning boy's head, which was now above, now under, the water. The next picture is of the top of the steps and the boy being rolled face downwards across a barrel to get the sea water out of him. Crude first aid, but effective.

It used to be fine for the boys to watch the old steam colliers come along from North Corner to tie up at the quay. The *Stobart* was one that frequently came. Sunderland was her port, I think, and I wonder if she is still afloat.

But long ago it was mast and sail that held an even greater attraction for boys. Timber ships, full rigged, used to come to Flathouse from Norway and other Scandinavian countries, manned by big blond seamen and loaded with sweet-smelling timber that filled the holds and overflowed in stacks on the decks. We used to go aboard cheekily without permission and play about the rigging. It was a 'dare' to reach the first crosstrees.

I learned on inquiry that to continue my walk along the foreshore towards Rudmore, I must go up again into Commercial Road and bypass the naval establishment. I did so and turned down Kettering Terrace to reach the sea again. Here I saw evidence of much greater activity than of old in the timber yards of Bailey and White. In fact I had not seen so much timber for years, and evidently being worked with the most modern machinery.

Continuing along the shore past the end wall of the old Mile End cemetery, memory was stirred again by a little wharf where, as a small boy, I first swam out of my depth. Most of us had no swimming instruction in those days and would progress from a dog paddle to breaststroke in shallow water just by trying. That same little quay brought another memory – that of a tragedy that still produces mixed feelings. A little chap bathing, but unable to swim, stood on the edge of a barge and shouted: 'See me dive.' He swung his arms over without meaning to and he was drowned. Relating the affair to his teacher in school next day a playmate told how he rushed off to break the news to the little chap's grandfather, with whom he lived. He said that he asked the grandfather if he had a boy named Fred. On being told yes he said: 'Well you ain't now cos he's bin drownded.' No one could accuse that boy of circumlocution.

Farther along and new to me was a concrete structure over a quay at which a small collier had just arrived to unload. Across the way was Whale Island and to my right the turning up into Rudmore with the Ship and Castle public house with its little 'hard' on the edge of the water. It was just the place to refresh oneself and to look out over the harbour.

Three old Rudmorians were leaning on the rail opposite the pub and with them I exchanged a few memories about Whale Island and when its bridge was built. Then up again into Commercial Road with its people and buses. I felt I had renewed acquaintance with a bit of Portsmouth and some of the people of it, both having a distinct and rather separate air about them.

A busy day at the Flathouse Quay as timber is unloaded from a German freighter.

The old Royal Yacht Victoria and Albert *looks to be in a sad and sorry state moored at Rudmore as* Britannia *comes into harbour behind her.*

The camera moves forward to 1955 and the Victoria and Albert *is towed away to her final resting place.*

The ornate pillars of the Mile End Cemetery were soon to disappear in the development of the city's ferry port. This picture is from the late 1950s.

A corner of the cemetery at Mile End. The burial grounds were levelled and the tombstones moved to form pleasant gardens – Mile End Gardens – that remained until 1978.

Ships of many different kinds berthed at Flathouse as this old sailing vessel which paid a visit in the 1930s shows.

In the old days Rudmore boasted its own windmill which was not used to produce flour but ground lime for buildings.

A view of Twyford Avenue in the 1930s with an eye-catching notice for Sydenham's timber firm displayed on the wall.

Traffic is very light in Commercial Road at Mile End in the 1960s before redevelopment of the city changed the view.

The ornate tracery of the Rudmore gasholder, a familiar sight in the area for many years. It was demolished in 1978 with the development of the ferry port.

Sydenham's timber firm can be seen to the right of this picture from the 1970s, which shows the new roundabout being built to link with the M275. The present-day flyover came later.

The old Ship & Castle public house boasted its own quay where customers and quay workers could have a drink and watch the shipping. A group of Rudmorians are enjoying the view.

The Market Place of Yesteryear

(First published 9 August 1951)

Weekends for many Portsmouth youngsters a couple of generations ago meant two things in particular. One was Sunday school; the other was Saturday evening in Charlotte Street. Two age-old gatherings of civilised man – the market place and the temple.

Charlotte Street! Who will forget the sights, the smells, the shouts and noises of that packed thoroughfare at the height of a Saturday evening's marketing. But there was usually a prelude at noon to the evening's excitement. That was at the Unicorn Gate, when the 'dockies' flocked out, free for the weekend. Along the old railway wall in springtime seedlings for their gardens could be cheaply bought, and much else including second-hand clothes.

But the centres of fun were the wagonettes of Sequah, the medicine man, and a certain coloured gentleman who sold some sort of dentifrice. Sequah, in his Wild West garb, was well known to a wider circle than Portsmouth. I remember particularly his Sequah's Mexican Oil for all aches and pains. 'R-r-r-rub it in the part affected!' he would shout in very impressive tones. He had the grand manner and presence of a born salesman.

The coloured gentleman with his wide grin showing teeth startlingly white against his black skin was even more a centre of interest and fun. He must have been the pioneer of free dental service in those pre-National Health days, for he would pull out teeth for nothing. Great was the joy of the callous crowd when some poor sufferer mounted the steps of the wagonette to have a tooth out. No cocaine, no gas. He just held tight while the struggle lasted and the crowd laughed and cheered, until with a still wider grin of triumph the coloured gentleman held aloft the forceps and the tooth. One can only guess what the patient felt. There was a typical dockyard legend that in difficult cases a rope was secured to the forceps and a crowd of mateys heaved on it to help the extraction!

But noon at the Unicorn Gate was just the prologue to the evening's play in Charlotte Street where the narrow street was packed solid with people from end to end. The old paraffin flares supplied light to the stalls, and the shouts of the sellers of fruit, vegetables and sweets and so on in the upper part of the street were deafening. Cheapness was the idea. There were oranges at Christmas time at 40 for a shilling, and straw-berries in season selling late in the evening at sixpence for a 7lb box.

There were always good boiled sweets at a penny a half pound – great mounds of them in cheerful colours on the stall of a firm named Duffy. There were stalls where a boy fond of reading could buy half a dozen 'bloods' bound together for about tuppence. There were, in the winter time, hot roast chestnuts sold by little dark Italians who never minded you having a warm in front of the cosy coke fire on wheels; and hot potatoes too, and green peas hot in gravy on a little plate, and of course, whelks and cockles in vinegar.

You could buy a pup or a kitten, chicks and chickens, tame mice or a tortoise, with advice as to their care thrown in.

And amid all the business and the hubbub, round the corner in a side street a Salvation Army band and hymn singing sometimes added an accompaniment to all the market sounds. It did not seem incongruous.

But the great attractions were the 'cheap-jacks' on their stands further down the street. Their wares were usually something for tuppence.

One loquacious chap of foreign blood used to sell great slabs of French nougat at tuppence a large lump, which he sawed off with a tremen-dous knife – the very grandfather of all carvers. When business flagged he used to burst suddenly into a loud and tragic speech, declaring life was vain and empty and he would end it all, finishing up with the great knife across his throat and shouting: 'I will now cut my' (a long pause) 'nougat!'

He immediately fell to sawing away at the nougat again with a happy grin on his face.

Another used to sell cardigans, and to prove his sincerity he used to assure the crowd that he wore one of the self-same cardigans himself, and peeling it off, he would offer to let them have that very one if they wished.

Later in the evening there were the butchers who Dutch-auctioned their remaining stacks of joints – real joints – to clear. A family-sized one went for a shilling or so, accompanied by good-natured quips and remarks for the buyer, who usually returned as good as she got. A stock joke from the butcher as he tossed a leg of mutton to the assistant who was weighing and wrapping was: 'Weigh up that lady's leg, Bill.' And the lady buyer, who was an expert in Charlotte Street repartee, would retort: 'And you ain't seen a finer one, mister!'

Down at the bottom end of the street there

would often be a solemn sort of gentleman in a frock coat, selling bottles of cure-all. He would carefully explain that he was not a doctor but, as carefully, imply that he knew much more about it than any doctor could. He would bring out some tremendous medical words and phrases which, I suspect, he understood about as well as his hearers did, and finally come down to selling his bottles.

Farther still down the street, where stalls were few and the flares and shouts were rare, were usually one or two dingy, dark and rather pathetic barrows holding heaps of old clothing, worn boots, old bicycle wheels, broken bits of

metal and perhaps a rusty old mangle. I often wondered who bought and who sold, for these poor heaps were on the edge of the outer darkness. I turned back with relief to the cheerful lights and noise.

Yes, Charlotte Street on a Saturday night was great fun for the youngsters and a chance for the housewives to make cheap purchases – and the husbands – who had to make a little money go a long way, but it was always a jolly expedition. There was so much more than buying and selling to it; so much of human nature in its intimate contacts; and often much good fun and hilarity.

The market at the Unicorn Gate at out-muster time was just a prelude to the fun to be had in Charlotte Street later in the day.

Charlotte Street market continued to operate even after German bombs had devastated much of the area.

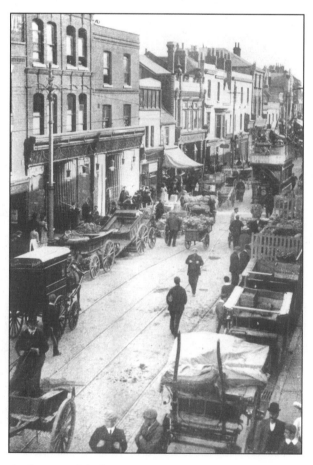

At the turn of the last century Commercial Road was like a vast market-place, its clutter of carts and barrows causing obvious difficulties for the tramcar.

Barrows of all shapes and sizes lined Commercial Road as goods were bought and sold.

The Classic cinema forms a background to the unloading of vegetables in Commercial Road. The shop fronts show names from the past, such as Weaver to Wearer and the Home and Colonial Stores. The classic opened in September 1936 as the Cinenews but changed its name in 1937 when this picture was taken.

This butcher in Castle Road, Southsea, was reaching for the sky with his display of poultry, a sight often to be seen at Christmas time.

The permanent stores were not above displaying their wares to leave no doubt to the shopper of what was on offer. Hartley's naval outfitters in Commercial Road offered uniforms of all shapes and sizes.

Quay Workers at the Camber

(First published 16 August 1951)

Turn down Oyster Street from High Street, or go down White Hart Row opposite Sally Port. Or take any turning on the right halfway down Broad Street. The names sound like something out of Captain Marryat, but the places are real enough.

Do just that and you come out on Portsmouth's Camber, and at once get an impression that has the smack of Cornish fishing village and a hint of London River.

You will see big colliers from the north-eastern coal ports being unloaded with the latest cranes and grabs; Dutch and French boats bringing crated vegetables and fruit; little smacks aboard which Bretons tie the familiar strings of onions; barges from the Isle of Wight landing crates and barrels of beer; launches, yachts and boats aplenty in being or in building at Vosper's yards.

Along the waterfront are big modern storage sheds, enormous coalbunkers with travelling cranes spanning them overhead, and harbour offices. On the quays are the dockers, the inevitable old-timers smoking shag, and the boys perched precariously on the edge, fishing hopefully, but not so patiently.

The Camber has changed a lot since then, and has lost some of its picturesqueness and gained in importance, in efficiency, and in extended use. The old group of buildings at Dirty Corner, and characteristic of the older Camber, are sadly mostly gone. The ancient maps and drawings of Old Portsmouth always show plainly this arm of the harbour, such a quiet little backwater tucked away out of the weather behind Spice Island.

James II in 1687, with only a year of his short unlucky reign to go, visited the spot to open the gate named after him. The gate is now the entrance to one of the services' recreation grounds. It used to stand across the end of Broad Street, by Sally Port, shutting Point outside the town. There was on the Camber wall by the Old White Hart Barracks the King's monogram in stone, but it seems to have gone now. The barracks are gone, too.

Outside the gate in Broad Street was a drawbridge over the narrow arm of water that used to connect sea and Camber. It is said that one desperate way of escaping press gangs was to dive into this ditch and swim into the Camber, climbing out somewhere to hide among the old streets and houses with the willing aid of their inhabitants.

Rough doings and rough times. Students of Portsmouth history have often found contemporary references to the men of bygone Portsmouth as a pretty hard-bitten lot. It seems clear that the

circumstances of their lives and times developed in them a far from soft sort of character. They were of the breed that fought at the Nile and at Trafalgar, and whom Nelson described as invincible. They could not afford to be milksops.

Certainly the men of the Camber and Point shared those qualities, to say the least, and still do. Boys from other parts of the town used to tread softly down that way, and never argued with the 'reglars'. These children were the sorts of material on which, long ago, John Pounds worked and poured out his compassionate heart. Education and general uplift have had their effect now, but Portsmouth and England can still do with people of strong and direct character. At Point and the Camber you get them.

The two sides of the Camber once were connected by a bridge, with a homely pub conveniently placed on the far side. Some years ago the bridge was cleared away and the passage widened to allow the entrance of bigger vessels and to give more quay space.

The smack of Cornish fishing village lessens, but a stronger hint of London River emerges in this old and still picturesque bit of Portsmouth.

A collier unloads her cargo in this evocative view from between the wars.

The Camber takes the foreground in this stunning aerial view from 1931. On the common, to the right of the picture, can be seen the tents and marquees of the Royal Counties Agricultural Show.

James II monogram, which used to be seen on the wall near the old White Hart Barracks.

Fishing boats are gathered together at the Camber with their nets hung out to dry between catches.

A French onion seller prepares his wares in time-honoured fashion at Old Portsmouth before going out to sell his wares around the streets of the city. This evocative picture was secured in 1932 when four boatloads of men arrived from Roscoff, near Brest, in August of that year.

Oyster Street was one of the tiny thoroughfares of Old Portsmouth around the Camber area, pictured here in 1932.

A smart selection of what would now be seen only at a rally of vintage vehicles forms an unusual tableau on the car ferry Fishbourne *in 1927.*

One of the quaint old buildings situated in Oyster Street. Workers from the Camber would have known these tiny streets well.

A lone motorcyclist makes his way down Highbury Street in the days when public houses were on every street corner. Although this view is from 1948 the street would have been recognisable 100 years before.

White Hart Row with some of its original buildings sadly awaiting demolition following the ravages of the Second World War.

In 1970 Oyster Street became the focus of an archaeological dig when the remains of a clay pipe factory were unearthed.

Cobbler John Pounds taught many a poor youngster from the Camber area at his tiny workshop and school in Highbury Street. This picture was taken in 1937.

The Citizen Sentries had Their Trials

(First published 2 October 1951)

In July 1914 soldiers stood on the walls of Southsea Castle and watched the fleet, after the review by King George V, proceeding to battle stations.

Winston Churchill, then First Lord, had prudently brought the fleet together. The weather was very hot that year, but the 'Saturday afternoon soldiers' in the castle found it not a bit warm sleeping in the arched recesses of the walls on three planks, with two blankets apiece. These 'blankets' were often lengths of suiting or travelling rugs given by the public to eke out the shortage of army blankets. (Who mentioned sheets and pyjamas, cots and bedside lamps!)

Watching 'rosy-fingered dawn' come up over the sea may previously have been for some of those young men a rare and romantic thing, but a month or two of manning an all-night searchlight alone in an emplacement made for more prosaic thoughts. Dawn was welcomed then with a yawn, and as a chance of 'getting the eye down'.

To add something to those early war months in the castle, a storm washed a great hole in the glacis sloping down to the sea, big enough to accommodate a couple of houses. To the joys of nights on the searchlights were added days of concrete mixing by hand and shoving barrows of shingle and cement, until even the clerical types grew horny palms. The place of their labour still shows plainly towards the eastern end of the glacis. They might quote Wren when he said: 'If you wish to see my monument, look around you.'

Sometimes a little spare time was spent in the moat, and exploring the damp underground passages that run round the moat under the glacis. But the days and nights were frequently made less dull by the presence of a detachment of a famous Highland infantry regiment who did guard duty around the castle. Those lads were – lads. Little fellows with a fierce pride. They were given the order to fall out for a spell just inside the gate, and immediately two who had apparently had some difference of opinion on the march, shed packs and rifles and were at each other in a flash.

They were indeed a famous fighting regiment, and were not averse to keeping their hands – or fists – in on each other if the common enemy was not available. On sentry-go in the dark they loved to let someone approach quite closely and unaware before barking out a sudden: 'Halt who goes there?' with a bayonet under the person's chin.

Sometimes one of them on duty at night on the west bank of the castle would *think* he saw a figure climbing the fence, and would let off a couple of enthusiastic rounds. There are more ways than one of varying the monotony of sentry duty!

Although in that war the blackout was not the complete thing we saw in 1939, there was often some little excitement over reports about lights flashing from top windows of houses across the common, or from spots on the common itself. The fear was presumably that German submarines were being signalled. Usually an armed patrol was sent out from the castle to investigate, with little faith in any need for the excursion. The only captures were courting couples who were usually not amused.

One man was brought in one night for some reason and was searched. He had a notebook full of strange hieroglyphics and nonsensical words. 'Secret code,' thought all and sundry. It was a long time before the poor chap could convince his questioners that he went in for competitions in a weekly magazine, and the jottings were his inspirations.

After the first phase of the 1914 war was over, Sir John French, as he then was, came from France to take the home command. He came to inspect the castle and its men and had kind words for the garrison on parade.

Many of the Portsmouth men who manned the old castle at the beginning of that war, went into other units and found themselves in other places much more uncomfortable than Southsea Castle, from France to India and many spots in between. Afterwards they took the chance to walk around the castle, cocking an eye that way with rather a proprietary feeling and even some affection.

Uppermost in their minds would have been memories of the lighter and more irresponsible side of those times. May Southsea Castle keep its quiet habit and never give rise to any memories more tragic than these.

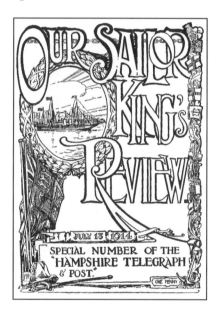

Special edition of the Hampshire Telegraph *issued as a souvenir of the 1914 fleet review.*

Southsea Castle is pictured between the wars with its distinctive lighthouse and water tower.

This view of Southsea Castle from the air clearly shows its distinctive shape. The lighthouse still remains but the old water tower has disappeared. This picture was taken before the construction of the D-Day museum close by.

Manning the searchlights at Southsea Castle was a mundane task given a more glamorous look by Portsmouth photographer Edgar Ward.

Glimpsing History Through the Gates

(First published 19 October 1951)

It is remarkable how in history and literature, religious and secular, gates have seized the imagination of men. Gates – those gaps in defence or wall, open to friends and barred and bolted against enemies.

It begins with the Gates of Eden in *Genesis*, and ends with the Pearly Gates in *Revelation*. Between that alpha and omega are gates innumerable, real or fanciful. There are the gates of Constantinople and of Troy, blood bespattered, and there is that memorable gate which had a chamber above it whence David looked out for his son Absalom, and in which he later mourned him in one of the most moving and beautiful passages of the Bible.

There is the Traitors' Gate at the Tower of London that closed behind so many tragedies. And Dante's awful gate of Hell cannot be forgotten, with its horrible inscription above – All hope abandon, ye who enter here. But there is also the gate of hope in Jerusalem, palm strewn, where once entered a humble ass and its rider. These are

but a few of the gates in the story of Man.

Portsmouth has its full share of gates, although less renowned. All but one of the city gates have been uprooted and put elsewhere, or are altogether gone.

The Landport Gate, main entrance to the older Portsmouth, stands where it stood where the ramparts crossed the end of High Street at Cambridge Junction. This one and the others must have been much more impressive in their heyday, flanked by grassy tree-topped ramparts and fronted by moat, ditch and glacis. It is true that we cannot now undo what our forefathers did a century or less ago, and laments are therefore useless. But what a showplace Old Portsmouth would have been, unique in its sort, if those old gates, ramparts and moats had been preserved.

The present Landport Gate dates from 1760, but for centuries before there had been gates on the spot. It was an earlier gate than this one at which Pepys placed a man to give notice of its closing at night when he was being entertained in the way he loved in the town, but was sleeping outside it.

Nelson, as a young officer, once came clattering through the present gate on the back of a runaway horse, which carried him right through the town, when he finally threw himself off to avoid worse injury. Sailors ashore seem to have a weakness for horse riding. That particular horse might have caused more loss to England than the wooden horse did to Troy.

Another of the gates of Old Portsmouth was King James's Gate. This is the one that once stood at the entrance to the recreation ground by the Victoria Hall. It is now in Burnaby Road on the other side of the same ground.

It was originally surmounted by a ball-topped dome of the sort still seen on the Landport Gate, flanked by two curved wings in Italian style. The present iron gates are of course modern additions.

The third gate was King William's Gate, erected in the 1830s, and taken down about forty years later. It had no pretence to beauty. This was the one that spanned what is now Pembroke Road, where the ramparts crossed it, and it was at this spot that Nelson and his horse parted company.

The Quay Gate, erected in the time of George II, was in the town wall and led out to the Camber. It was a fine gate, judging from pictures, but nothing of it remains.

In Queen Anne's time, in the early-eighteenth century, Portsea began to grow up to house dockyard workers and the fortifications were extended from Old Portsmouth. In these new ramparts other gates were placed, the best known being the Lion Gate at the end of Queen Street by Lion Terrace, and the Unicorn Gate near the bottom end of North Street.

The Lion Gate is now in the dockyard at the base of the new Semaphore Tower, and there is still a Unicorn Gate to the dockyard not far from the old site.

I once could walk from the bottom of North Street and turn to the left down a very quiet lane – Anchor Gate Lane. There, at the end of the old Portsea ramparts, used to be the Anchor Gate. There was a prison there, and gangs of convicts were often seen wheeling a truck and sweeping the road by the black wooden walls of the dockyard. All this area is now walled off into the dockyard, and Portsea boys cannot, as they used to, find a quiet playground 'round the walls'.

Apart from all these gates, which were exits and entrances to the older Portsmouth, the city has many worth the study of those who delight in the work of men's hands. There is the old Queen Anne, main gate of the dockyard, and the other gates of the same: the gate of the naval barracks, of Victoria Barracks and Eastney Barracks, and others too.

Many gates there are, and many are they, humble and great, who have passed through them. It needs little imagination to picture that long procession down the years.

The familiar main gate of the dockyard is decorated for the Jubilee of George V and Queen Mary. Delivery boys wait to enter the yard while workers make their way homewards.

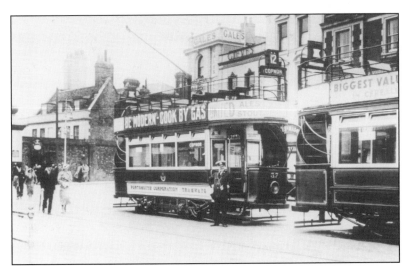

The main gate at the Hard was a major changeover point for the trams. Number 12 service terminated at Copnor.

The Lion Gate was built in 1770 and originally stood at the eastern end of Queen Street. It was demolished in 1871 and the pieces were stored for future use. When the Semaphore Tower was rebuilt following the 1913 fire the Lion Gate was built into its base, as this picture shows.

The picture from about 1875 shows an unusual view of the Lion Gate in its original position, with the camera situated on the inside of the walls, looking outwards.

King James's Gate was built in 1687 and stood at the end of Broad Street, Old Portsmouth. It was partly re-erected as an entrance to the officers' recreation ground.

Quay Gate was erected in 1734 and stood near the Camber.

The Landport Gate, the only one to survive in its original position.

Other gates include the Marlborough Gate, one of the entrances to the dockyard.

This view of Edinburgh Road, showing the barracks gateway in 1970, has changed significantly from the following picture.

The gateway to the Royal Naval barracks where stone taken from the old Quay Gate was used in its construction.

Pembroke Road in slower days with the Cathedral spire in the distance. King William's Gate once stood at the spot from where this picture was taken.

Princes Drank to the People Here

(First published 26 May 1952)

If there is one spot among many in old Portsmouth where one would wish to borrow and use H.G. Wells's time machine, it is that quiet place with its immediate surroundings known as Governor's Green.

Unless there are a few youngsters at football on the green, it is now an even quieter spot than it was a generation or more ago. But it is in the very long ago that most of its story lies. Somewhere in front of that long railing that runs from the Royal George gun along the parade ground and the green, a crowd of angry unpaid soldiers and sailors beat a bishop to death. Not so quiet a spot then!

Today the Garrison Church can boast a roof over only its chancel. This chancel was the original chapel of the old Domus Dei – God's house – and the present nave served other purposes.

God's house was a hospital in the broad, older sense of the word. Some time in the reign of King John, before he sealed Magna Carta, the Bishop of Winchester founded this hospital with a master and brethren to look after twelve poor aged men, and to assist travellers, pilgrims and the sick. It was not a great many years after Thomas à Becket had been murdered and qualified as a saint, and it is likely that some overseas pilgrims, landing at Portsmouth and bound for his tomb at Canterbury, were welcomed and refreshed at Domus Dei.

The foundation apparently did good work for very many years. Its buildings occupied much of the half of Governor's Green nearest Grand Parade. The good work had been going on for more than two centuries when the murder referred to, of Bishop Moleyns of Chichester, took place. It was in 1450, in the troubled days when England was as a bone coveted by two dogs – the Wars of the Roses. Presumably the bishop was staying at Domus Dei having been sent to try to quiet the disgruntled soldiers. He was haranguing the crowd outside the gates, and was killed there.

The displeasure and punishment of the Church was inflicted on the town. For more than fifty years Portsmouth appeared to suffer much trouble, and finally the townspeople in penance, built a chapel on the fatal spot. Nothing visible remains of this chapel, but one wonders what could be unearthed hereabouts by a little digging.

It was not a great many years after the building of this chapel that Henry VIII closed Domus Dei at the time of the Dissolution of the Monasteries. It had done its good work for three centuries or more, in times when the welfare state was far in the future. The master was made Dean of St Paul's for complying with the King's demands; being more discreet than some other heads of old foundations, who were hanged for not being so accommodating.

After the closing, the buildings were used for a period to store munitions of war. Finally in Queen Elizabeth's time the place was converted into a residence for the military governors of the town – hence Governor's Green. It served this purpose until 1827. In those two or three centuries two events stand out among many. The first was the marriage of Charles II to the Portuguese princess Catherine of Braganza. The Garrison Church possessed an altar-cloth embroidered with a picture of Lisbon and the Portuguese royal arms, a souvenir of that marriage.

The second event is still commemorated for all to see, on the green just beyond the east end of the church. There on the old site stands an old mortar. In 1814 the Allies were celebrating as they thought the downfall of Europe's arch-enemy Napoleon had occurred. Trafalgar had crippled him nine years before, and the Peninsula War and his tragic Russian campaign of 1812 had exhausted him. He was to surprise all his enemies a year after this gathering of 'captains and kings' at Portsmouth, by escaping from Elba and making his last bid at Waterloo where Wellington mastered him.

Lord Frederick FitzClarence did much for Portsmouth. The citizens showed their gratitude by erecting the pillar in the gardens opposite Victoria Barracks. Clarence Parade and Clarence Pier bear his name. It was because of him that the esplanade from the Hot Walls to the castle, along the edge of the then swampy common, was constructed – a great asset to the infant Southsea.

Richard Esmond charmingly illustrated the old mortar outside the Garrison Church.

The Garrison Church pictured in the peaceful days before the Great War when it still had its roof.

The splendid interior of the Garrison Church pictured before the blitz of 1941 took its toll.

The old saluting battery at Old Portsmouth pictured in the popular Spithead series of postcards.

Grand Parade in focus in pre-war days with a handful of stately cars parked in the centre, and a water tower high above the buildings in High Street.

A popular Sunday event for residents and visitors was the Army Church Parade at the Garrison Church. The parades were often recorded by cameramen – this image is from about 1900.

The Garrison Church still stands proudly in this post-war view taken on what is obviously a damp day.

The camera captures another view of Grand Parade in the balmy days of the 1930s. A plaque on the house in Pembroke Road where Vicat Cole once lived recalls a great artist.

The Old Street Sellers Offered a Strange Assortment

(First published 3 June 1952)

Gone in this modern life that seems to iron out individuality are many Portsmouth 'types'. There was a well-known character of the early 1890s known as 'Nosy' Burrows, who used to go around with a tray slung about his shoulders selling oranges and nuts in the streets and pubs. He was truly a character and might in other circumstances have made much of his life, for he had a very ready and caustic wit, an obvious love of words, and the ability to put much of what he said immediately into rhyme.

He talked much, and in the grand manner. He sold in rhyme, and sometimes passed cutting remarks in rhyme about those who upset him.

His most precious possession was the broad belt that carried his tray. It was a gift to him from Queen Victoria, in return for a poem he sent her on her jubilee. The belt was inscribed across the front to that effect.

The Sunday afternoon streets of old were quiet. Grown-ups were probably snatching forty winks while the children were at Sunday school. But coming somehow naturally in the remembering of that Sabbath quiet are the cries of the sellers of winkles and watercress. Winkles at twopence a pint, and watercress at a 'penny an 'andful' – either or both for Sunday high tea.

There was one watercress seller who used to tramp the streets of the older parts of Portsmouth. He was a little man with ginger whiskers and a quick jerky walk, bent well over his barrow as he pushed it. We used to hear tales of him – that he had once been rich and had gambled away all his wealth and had come down to a 'penny an 'andful'.

Familiar too was the muffin bell, rung in rhythm with the steps of the muffin man. He carried the tray on his head, with a thick pad of what looked like dough to soften the load. He walked quite upright because of his tray, like Eastern women with their water jars, and never dropped the tray, although we children watched and possibly hoped for it.

Good Friday comes and goes now for most of us like any other public holiday. Gone is another of the marks of that other life before the wars when enterprising boys with a basket full of cold 'hot cross buns' got up early and filled the streets with their cries, and their pockets with coppers.

In one part of Portsmouth lived 'Hot-pie' Johnson, who carried on his arm a sort of portable oven containing hot meat pies at a penny each. The wits in the bar of a certain pub used to start a chorus of 'meows' as he came in to sell, but nevertheless the pies were very tasty.

There was a tall blind man with a frock coat and top hat who used to come tapping along the street with his stick, crying: 'Bluebottle and flies, catch 'em alive.' He sold flypapers and had one as a sample wrapped around his hat – an obvious graveyard for the insects.

A strange pathetic little man used to call at front doors selling *Old Moore's Almanac*. There was a story, probably only a legend, that he was well-off, but he often begged 'a little bit of tea' from his customers.

The cry of: 'Any chairs for mending', was often heard, and along would come the little man, always with one old chair on his arm, and a bunch of cane or reed. As a child I used to wonder whose chair it was.

With the cry of: 'Cat's meat and dog's meat', the little cart of the cat's meat man would appear. He usually had a little following of felines down the street as though he were a sort of Pied Piper to the hunters instead of the hunted.

Hokey-pokey then was ice cream. It was not the product of big business as it is now, but was made by Italian families in Portsea and in the little ways off Charlotte Street. The sellers were all named Joe, at least by their customers who seldom spent more than a ha'penny. The gaily-painted carts were an outpouring of Latin exuberance. The main motif was usually portraits of the Italian royal family, the whole painted in oils and a great pride to their owners.

The box-like barrow contained two zinc cylindrical containers with lids of polished brass. In one was the usual vanilla variety and in the other a sort of watery frozen concoction flavoured with lemon. The children liked to clamber up on the wheel hubs and put their noses as near as possible to the containers while being served. The measure was ladled out on a wooden spoon and scraped on to a piece of paper. Alternatively they could have it in a cone-shaped glass, so thick that dropping it could do no harm. Biscuit wafers and cones came later on – a modern refinement.

These people and their businesses once made the streets of Portsmouth a little more colourful and interesting. In the case of some of them, it is blessing that conditions have so altered that they are no longer seen. For the others, they remain pleasant memories of the older different life of Portsmouth, and a link with a still older England when street cries and street sellers were part and parcel of everyday life.

Richard Esmond remembers the muffin man in his charming little sketch of old-time life in Orange Street, Portsea.

Salt Airs Add Spice to the Southsea Holiday

(First published 24 July 1952)

Southsea is different! The reason? Because Portsmouth, Spithead, the harbour and the Navy are inseparable from it.

Southsea visitors are hardly to be expected to return home wearing bell-bottomed trousers and with a passion for dancing the hornpipe and splicing the mainbrace, although that last is not difficult. But they may at least go home with a slight nautical flavour about them, in addition to a nice tan.

They could, for instance, when they brave the waves on some of the many steamer trips, correct some of the landlubbers' errors that make the sailorman smile. One doesn't go upstairs or downstairs on a ship, but up on deck or below. The chimney is not a chimney but a funnel. The sharp end of a ship, as the lady called it, is the bow, the other the stern. There are no rooms on a ship (even if passenger boats have saloons) but cabins.

Sometimes in leaving the pier a steamer goes astern, but never backwards or in reverse; and when clear, she goes ahead, not forward. When facing ahead, the left is the port side and the right the starboard. As for windward and leeward, they are best explained by the story of the old sailor who, when questioned as to which was which, said: 'If you stands to leeward of me when I spits, it's your own fault.'

There are no floors on a ship, but decks. There is no kitchen, but a galley. In my young days, flavoured by naval associations, a stone jam jar was always called a galley-pot. One boards a ship by gangway or brow. Those are just a few ship words for the Southsea visitor to absorb with Southsea air.

But when the visitor views the Navy, or goes aboard the *Victory*, as all ought to do, he is likely to be more at sea, in both senses, than ever, for Navy language is a thing apart. That last statement is perhaps ambiguous. To illustrate one possible meaning of it, *Punch* years ago printed a drawing of a party of sailors doing paintwork on the quarterdeck. One had upset his pot of paint on the deck! An officer was asking the petty officer in charge all about it. 'What on earth did you say to him?' he asked. The petty officer, bravely and wildly improvising said: 'I says to him, sir, I says, "My goodness what *has* you done"?' Decidedly an understatement.

Only those who are acquainted with what the quarterdeck means in the Navy, and who can imagine what the petty officer really did say to the matelot, can probably appreciate that story.

Visitors to a Royal Navy vessel may see the usual salute given by all ranks on stepping on to the quarterdeck. This is usually thought to be a salute to the deck associated with commissioned officers. It is more likely a relic of the days, centuries ago, when a usual feature of this part of the ship was a crucifix.

If a Navy man is heard addressing a shipmate as Nobby, the latter's surname is certainly Clark. Millers are always Dusty, and a Martin always answers to Pincher. It is difficult to say why. Tiny or Shorty is seldom less than six feet.

Various sections of a naval ship's company are known by nicknames, according to their duties. There was a Navy man, many years ago, who introduced a shipmate to his wife as 'old bunting tosser'. Great was the joy later when the lady politely addressed the chap in the signals as Mr Bunting Tosser.

The usual three masts to be seen on such ships as the *Victory*, visitors will learn to know as fore, main, and mizzenmasts, going from bow to stern. They can acquaint themselves on the *Victory* with such items as bowsprit, and the ports out of which peep the old muzzle loaders. Further, to the names of any of the maze of rigging aloft, they will hardly want to go, for that is to be truly nautical in a bygone sense, and hardly necessary now even for Navy men.

Yes, indeed, Southsea is different. It has ample joys for the visitor, but there is in addition, so much of interest beyond the low water mark.

In Victorian times people flocked to the beach to see the ships pass. This crowd gathered near Clarence Pier to cheer the Royal Yacht Victoria and Albert *as she made her way out of harbour.*

Day-trippers at Southsea leave their coach and pose somewhat self-conciously for the camera in the times when such a journey to the seaside was still a rarity. Who they were, or where they were from, must remain a mystery as the original photograph provides no details.

Taking the sun on a convenient seat or strolling along the esplanade has always been an important facet of the Southsea holiday though some prefer to keep their coats on!

Even in wartime, with gas masks over the shoulder, the esplanade attracted a great number on a sunny day.

Crowds thronged to the beach in 1947 to see HMS Vanguard bring King George VI and Queen Elizabeth home from their South African tour.

Watching the great warships pass near Clarence Pier was a popular pastime. Here people stop to watch HMS Formidable as she passes the Esplanade.

A trip across the harbour could be rewarding for ship spotters when the might of the Royal Navy was in town. This picture shows the huge bulk of HMS Vanguard alongside at the South Railway Jetty.

Sally Port at Old Portsmouth was always a good view-point to see the ships. This spectator has parked his bike to stop to watch the submarine HMS Acheron enter harbour.

A chance to see the ships and meet the men was on offer at Portsmouth Navy Weeks.

Fleet reviews were a grand way to see the might of the Navy gathered together. This picture – one half of a stereoscopic pair produced by Underwood & Underwood in Washington, USA – shows the Royal Yacht Victoria and Albert passing through the fleet during the 1902 Coronation Review.

A boat trip offered a day out on the briny for many visitors. The paddle-steamer Merstone *kicks up 'ginger beer' as she manoeuvres into position to disembark her passengers in 1936.*

Boats of a much smaller kind could be enjoyed at the Canoe Lake where young and old could lose their 'landlubber' tag for an hour or so.

It was not always 'Sunny Southsea', as this picture of rough weather battering the esplanade shows.

Battered Portsea Keeps Memories Intact

(First published 16 August 1952)

Portsea was born of the dockyard, for two centuries or more lived mainly by it, and finally received its almost fatal wounds because of its proximity to it.

It was once an almost self-contained little town. In it lived the Navy and the dockyard people and many members of the business classes.

Portsea's story, compared with that of Old Portsmouth, is a short one. It might be considered in the modern jargon to be an overspill from the older place. It was very early in the eighteenth century that dockyard workers began to build homes for themselves on the area outside the Old Portsmouth fortifications known as Portsmouth Common. The earliest houses were those in the Bonfire Corner district.

It was not easy even then to build necessary homes, for authority then, as now, had something to say. The then governor of Portsmouth thought that to build up this area might endanger the defences of Old Portsmouth and the dockyard, and he even threatened to knock down with the gun of the garrison any buildings erected there.

The dockyard men eventually appealed to Queen Anne through her husband Prince George of Denmark, and royal consent was eventually given. The new main street was named Queen Street in honour of her majesty.

Portsmouth, because it has always been a service city, has always reflected national events more than most places, and one aspect of this is seen in its street names. Those of Portsea reveal completely its period in history. Mafeking, Pretoria and Kimberley roads in the eastern part of the city tell of their building during or soon after the South African War. Trafalgar, Copenhagen and Nile streets in Landport were begun in Nelson's days. There are many other examples. In the case of Portsea the street names read like a summary of eighteenth-century history. Prince George Street perpetuated the name of Queen Anne's husband. Marlborough Row, now within the dockyard, was a reminder of Mr Churchill's great ancestor, and Orange Street was named not after the fruit but the royal house of Orange and William III. Union Street speaks of the union of England and Scotland, and Hanover

Street of another royal house, while Hawke Street and Camden Alley recalls admiral and statesman of those days. Union Street, by the way, was the Hampshire Terrace of yesterday, for it was the street of lawyers.

Yet, although Portsea in the 1890s undoubtedly contained one or two plague spots in common with most seaports, it was for the most part a community of worthy naval and dockyard families who lived soberly in the old Queen Anne and Georgian houses and streets. These streets had not perhaps the mellowness of Old Portsmouth, but they certainly had charm and character of their own. Such places as St George's Square and Lion Terrace contained the handsome and dignified residences of important citizens.

However, Portsmouth grew, and the great outward movement of population began, and still goes on.

There was a closer-knit life of the smaller Portsmouth; the old houses that boasted no forecourts or front gardens, the attics, and the cellars which held the coal, such as the one where I went with feigned boldness with bigger brother to bring up the coal, and sometimes singed my hair with the candle flame as I bent to shovel the coal, for my eyes were fearfully searching the dark corners of the cellars instead of attending to the candle.

There were the quiet streets where it was possible to play marbles without fear of traffic. Perhaps Hamburg Square – Humbug Square to the boys – will be a name to bring a grin to some older lips. It was a quiet square off Daniel Street, quiet because it was formed of only the backs of houses. There, the boys of the neighbouring school always went when a difference had to be settled in the old fistic way, and that seemed fairly frequently.

Queen Street in its heyday, bright with shops of all sorts was a sight. Some of these shops today have the same names above as they had sixty years ago. There was a painful procession through that same street, when in about 1894, a particularly hard winter with prolonged frost drove unemployed building workers to parade with banners and collecting boxes.

And since houses and streets are nothing if not the homes and ways of men, prominent personalities come to mind. There was Dr Colt of Lion Terrace, who attended the entry into the world of who knows how many citizens of Portsmouth. He was a small sharp man, and with his carriage, top hat, and frock coat, and his black bag, he typified the medical man of that day. Another was Alderman Emanuel, a benevolent representative of his race and a noted mayor of Portsmouth.

There were others in plenty, for Portsea, like Old Portsmouth, produced characters in those days.

Union Street was traditionally the home of lawyers in late-Victorian and Edwardian days.

Queen Street – the main thoroughfare from the dockyard to the town centre – was once a bustling array of shops. The street is decorated here for the visit of the French fleet in August 1905.

What a contrast! A battered Queen Street looks desolate and sad in the aftermath of the Second World War.

The once crowded market of Charlotte Street was also left with a much changed face after the war.

One of the small roads, Pye Street, has a bleak air about it after the wartime bombing.

The Guildhall was almost destroyed in the war, and the ruins had to be fenced off as a safety measure.

Camden Alley was one of the old streets of Portsea which disappeared in the big clear-up after the war.

Portsmouth's Ancient and Attractive Neighbour

(First published 4 September 1952)

Portsmouth and its near neighbours make an area of almost endless study and recollection for me, for few places even in these days of accelerated building have changed and spread so much.

Portchester is an outstanding example of this for the name now calls up two very different pictures in the mind. The first is the modern spreading growth of new houses and bungalows spilling down the slope of Portsdown and across the main road even to the sea. The other picture is of the Portchester of old, a village hoary with age, mellow with years, older even than Portsmouth.

Today a smart bus took me rapidly along tarmac roads to the new Portchester, and the whole route is a built-up area.

Old Portchester was a small cluster of houses on the main road and a mile-long street, Castle Street, leading in quiet and increasing charm to the climax of the castle at its end. The back windows of the houses on the left side of Castle Street looked out over a fine prospect to the creek, Paulsgrove and the hill, and away down the harbour. The gardens then, as now, seemed to produce a great many apples. In fact, if the old village had considered a coat of arms, a castle supported by a clay pipe and an apple would have been appropriate.

Those who value and love old places, with their refreshing irregularity and variety in building, so pleasing to the eye and to the appreciative mind, must be thankful that old Portchester's long street and castle are so near the shore that modern development cannot surround and obliterate them. This is not by any means to decry modern development and the building of very necessary houses, but there must be few people who would not agree to the careful preservation of such specimens of bygone England as the old village.

Fortunately, Castle Street, at any rate from White Hart Lane to the castle, is unspoiled. A peep through the castle gate shows that the grounds are even better cared for than of old. A walk around the outside of the walls brings evidence of similar care, for the grass is kept very well, even up to the base of the walls. Some who remember back far enough will recall the great keep with a thick coat of ivy. It was cut down in about 1900, and a section of one of the great stems from the base of the keep was exhibited in a shop window at Kingston Cross.

Portchester long ago used to be a favourite spot for outings from Portsmouth, both private and of the Sunday school sort. The long crocodile of children detraining at the station would creep along the whole length of Castle Street to the castle grounds, where they were furnished with tea in a wooden building just inside the gate.

The guardians of the castle were the Russells acting on behalf of Squire Thistlethwaite of Southwick. The connection between Southwick and Portchester goes back through the centuries to Norman times when the monks, builders of the church within the castle, left Portchester for Southwick.

A few doors along on the same side, from the new public house near the castle, used to be an older pub well remembered for a satisfying lunch for the rambler – a big crust of new bread with a lump of cheese to match, and a pint of shandy-gaff. The total cost was 4d. Nearly opposite was a cottage where in the front room sat a lady, well known to visitors and respected by all. She was a very large lady but even more large-hearted and kind. Often she was seen in the castle gateway helping the Russells with their visitors. Her name was Durant, one of the Portchester names that suggest French origin from the times of the Napoleonic wars, when the castle held hundreds of French prisoners. No memories of old Portchester seem complete without mention of her.

For people who delight in antiquity, in old houses and cottages which are in many cases older in structure than their Georgian fronts would indicate, and who delight in the creek and boating, old Portchester must be an attractive place of residence. Many of its inhabitants are sure of it.

The road into Portchester between the wars. The boats are still moored at the old oil depot, and the traffic on the highway is extremely minimal.

Victorian children have a break from play to take a camera call outside Portchester's New Inn – with its famous ivy-covered walls – at the foot of Castle Street.

The land gate of Portchester Castle complete with the quarters of the custodian tacked on the ancient walls.

This view is only slightly changed today. The trees are gone and the car would be a modern vintage, but the scene through the water gate is certainly recognisable.

The ivy which once covered much of Portchester Castle keep is remembered by Richard Esmond.

Portchester foreshore is still a popular place for walkers and sightseers, although the view northward towards Portsdown Hill is now very different. This scene was recovered in the mid 1950s.

Leigh's clay pipe factory was situated at the top of Castle Street, and even today pieces of pipe can be dug up in many village gardens. Here a worker – often itinerant – moulds pipes.

Although the old Wicor windmill was demolished in the 1920s, the remains of the smaller mill along the foreshore can still be seen, although now it now stands on private land.

The Eastern Edge of Our Enchanting Island

(First published 30 September 1952)

Walking for pleasure seems out of date. Nevertheless blackberry time, even if no blackberries are picked, is the pleasantest walking time.

The crisp early autumn air, the sunshine that is never so golden as in September, and the sky which is never more blue throughout all the year, give an invitation that cannot be resisted by those who have the time and energy to respond.

There are plenty of enjoyable walks in Portsmouth and most of them give a sight of the sea. One, which is not so well known as it deserves to be, runs along the eastern shore of this island.

The walk should begin at Milton locks, and after turning left along the shore from there the only signpost to heed is the edge of Langstone harbour, which is followed almost all the time.

After leaving the locks, the walk by the water will, as like as not, not produce the sight of another human being until the back of St James's Hospital is left behind. The calm water across to Hayling is usually dotted with boats, and it would be hard to imagine a more pleasant setting or more secure anchorage for them.

The water is left for a short spell to round the Good Companions, which looks down Velder Avenue. Here the Eastern Road has to be followed for a short distance until the shore can be gained again, where the amphibious homes of

the enterprising people, who are determined on a home of their own, come into view.

From the houseboats onward, the path follows every turn of the coastland, here is the finest part of the walk, and here are the fresh air and wide views. Across the wide stretch of Langstone, the eye can rest in flatness and distance. Farlington and Bedhampton lie beyond the free stretch of water, and farther again, blue with distance, the hills of Goodwood. Below the sea wall the fast-moving traffic on the Eastern Road gets glimpses of the view, but full appreciation needs the stillness and quiet of the shore.

The square old house planted by the water's edge ahead is now a place of refreshment, opposite the golf course. Long ago it was privately occupied and was lonely and difficult to come at. Only a narrow unfrequented road from Milton, winding along near the shore, served it, with another, equally narrow and lonely, that wandered across Great Salterns from Copnor crossing, before Copnor boasted a bridge. The road went by way of Baffins Pond, then just another country pond, out across the salterns, where the seagulls flew undisturbed.

The old house will mark the end of a long enough walk for the most, and a bus can be boarded in the road below for the return. Hardier souls will continue along the quiet shore even as far as the bridge, where there are the beginnings of an enthusiastic sailing club. Even farther, the blackberries of Farlington Marshes will remind the walker of younger days.

The new Eastern Road has made this area more easily available, as if to compensate for the loss of old blackberrying haunts that used to serve Portsmouth boys. Hayling Island was one before the golf course was enclosed. There used to be the added attraction of the trip across in a big rowboat. The boatman was a stout blue-jerseyed man with a face burned by the Langstone sun to a depth of tan that would make the Hollywood variety look pale.

Another old expedition was to Browndown, through Gosport, another ha'penny water trip and a much longer walk. The aim was the boast of a whole gallon of blackberries in the basket. Fronds of bracken were laid over the berries for the journey home. The 'gallon' was often the generous estimate of youth and enthusiasm, like the size of the angler's fish. The tang of the blackberries, the turf and the bracken at Farlington will recall the blackberries gathered long ago in vanished Septembers.

Baffins Pond was a country retreat for town dwellers in the peaceful days of the past.

Some of the houseboats that provided living space of a different kind for many people along the eastern shore near Velder Creek. Many houseboats remained until fairly recently.

Ship ahoy! Flags and an awning provide a great setting for a picnic at one of the houseboats. This evocative scene was captured by the photographer in the 1920s.

The wide-open spaces of the eastern edge of Portsea Island pictured in the early 1930s, with the road winding across from Copnor.

Copnor railway crossing that was later replaced by Copnor Bridge in the early part of the twentieth century.

Velder Creek is packed with vessels of all kinds.

The unfinished Eastern Road became the venue for motor racing, bringing spectators in from all around the area. Portsmouth catered for enthusiasts by closing the road for the events, which were regularly held for a number of years in the 1930s.

Work stopped on the Eastern Road at the outbreak of war leaving it as the 'road to nowhere.'

The Eastern Road was completed after the war, although this view shows that it carried considerably less traffic than today!

Wymering – A Place Which Grew up with England

(First published 25 November 1952)

The future belongs to the young – who have little past. The older of us, who have little future, but much past, may be forgiven if we sometimes dwell in that past, and delight in the enchantment borne of its distance.

Much is heard one way or another of the new growths, which have appeared on Portsmouth's northern edge in the past forty or fifty years. Some of them have unfortunately, though of necessity, submerged such little and ancient communities as Wymering.

There was, for instance, the narrow turning out of Cosham High Street into the Portchester road. The old Swan Inn was not set back at the corner as is the new one. From there to Wymering was a country road, nothing on the northern side but the fields sloping up to Portsdown Hill, and little on the other until the farm and farm buildings opposite the church were reached. It was a quiet walk – no pavements, no people, and almost no traffic.

Wymering, now regarded perhaps as a junior brother to Cosham, was for centuries legally and ecclesiastically Cosham's father. At the time of Domesday, Wymering was a royal manor, and the records give complete enough accounts of its history thereafter. The spelling of the name varies through the centuries from Wimeringe through Wemering and Wymerynnge to the final Wymering, the spellings typical of the centuries concerned, and suggestive of the old freedom in spelling which some schoolboys still see no point in surrendering.

We read among many details of a thirteenth-century William de Fortibus, Earl of Albermarle, holding the manor from Henry III, and of it reverting to the crown later when Edward I gave it to his mother Eleanor. This de Fortibus, it is interesting to note, made a yearly gift of three-quarters of corn, valued at 15 shillings (a lot of money then) to the master and brethren of Domus Dei in Portsmouth, as a charge on the manor of Wymering. Domus Dei was then a fairly new foundation.

For centuries Wymering was closely connected to the Priory of Southwick. The gift of the living of Wymering was in the hands of the priory until the latter was closed by Henry VIII in the sixteenth century. The vicars of Wymering from then until 1817 were chosen by the lord of the Manor of Southwick. Later the Thistlethwaites, squires of Southwick, and Winchester College alternately, did so, until the gift passed into other hands. As late as 1894 Wymering was amalgamated with Widley to form the new parish of Cosham.

The church itself with its walls of Portsdown flint, does not give an impression of great age, but the oldest parts nevertheless, go back eight hundred years. Until 1860 there was a low square tower at the western end. In that year it was taken down and the present small bell tower erected. The large spread of tiled roof covers centre and side aisles in one span. Inside striking features are the slenderness of the pillars upholding the heavy arches, and the size of the chancel.

The church and vicarage, and the manor house on the other side of Wymering Lane, with farm and its buildings of flint still remaining, and a few cottages, made up the total of the Wymering village of old. Here was really peace not so long ago, the only traffic noises were the clop of horses' hooves and the sound of the iron-rimmed wheels, the quiet of the church and churchyard undisturbed.

Vicarage and manor house are both very old, but have been much altered over the years. The church and its immediate surroundings still indeed form an oasis of real Old England amid twentieth-century traffic and bricks and mortar.

It is still pleasant to come from the newness of the modern streets between Cosham and Wymering and suddenly shed the years at this old spot. It has altered little since an April day in 1906 when a friend and I sat in rural peace by the church, each busy with a sketchbook.

The grass verges of the road have given way to stone kerbs, the road is no longer dusty, and a graceful tree which grew by the gate near the corner of the churchyard is gone; otherwise that small scene is as it was. It is well worth much effort to keep it so, for it's the evidence that Wymering, far from being a mere housing estate, is a place which grew up with England – a place with a pedigree.

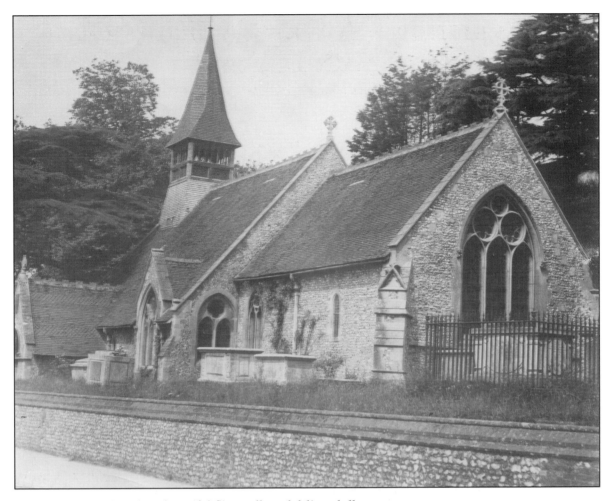

Wymering Church with its beautiful flint walls and delicate bell tower.

Nearby is Wymering Manor, historic building parts of which date from Elizabethan times. In the cellars are massive flint foundations, possibly of Roman or Saxon origins.

Memories of a Victorian's School Days

(First published 17 December 1952)

The scene was a busy shopping street at noon in Portsmouth. Plenty of traffic and many shoppers, but I was interested only in a big policeman and many small children.

The officer was shepherding the children from a nearby infants' school in batches across the dangerous road. The youngsters skipped happily up to the policeman, and many trustfully clutched his hand to cross, and having arrived waved their hands to him in pretty thanks and farewell. It was this that particularly struck me. 'When I was that age,' I mused, 'a policeman was someone to run from, not to!'

As it happened, the very day before, I had been rummaging in a drawer of my desk and had come across a little faded photo. It was a school group of about sixty years ago. In a corner of the picture was a little boy of five or so, with a round face and untidy hair, in the sailor jumper very commonly worn then. He was grinning widely, maybe in knowing disbelief at the photographer's usual story of the little bird in the camera. On the back of the photo was stamped 'E.B.A. Muspratt, Somers Road, Southsea, Portrait Painter and Photographer.'

I found it hard to identify myself with the child in the photo; and now the sight of the youngsters of today, and the thought of their light and airy schools, their little chairs and tables to fit little legs and bodies, the curriculum that provided for both bodily and mental activity, the children's obvious light-heartedness, their liking of school, all made me think of what an infant school used to be like as I remembered it. I thought that these are indeed the good days for children, and rejoiced to think so; even though some may think things are getting almost too easy for them.

In those days free movement was unheard of, indeed impossible, and discipline strict. (Discipline in the old sense) for babies! Normal posture when not writing or reading (writing on slates on the knee) was either 'hands behind and touch elbows' with chin up (the higher the chin the better the behaviour!) or 'fold arms'. Knuckles were rapped not only for misbehaviour, but for inability in lessons. Serious naughtiness got a dreaded punishment. In the passage by the side of the gallery was a door leading into the darkness under the gallery. There the coal and wood were stored and there in solitary confinement and total darkness a 'bad boy' was sometimes put for a spell.

It is not pleasant to think of the possible effect of that on a sensitive child. Perhaps those who were so treated were not the sensitive sort. Perhaps it is not fair to judge those responsible by present-day thought. Certainly the 'governess' is remembered as a kind, pretty woman, a good teacher in the manner and under the conditions of her time, and the school was accounted a good one in its day.

The curriculum for those children of from three to six years, was little more than the Three Rs, with sewing and knitting (even the boys knitted and sewed hems) and scripture. There was no learning by playing, no gentle introduction in the way of counting games, and none of the modern 'self-expression' and freedom. Letters and tables and spelling were hammered in by constant repetition. Adding, subtracting and the mysteries of 'borrowing' were learned by countless examples worked on slates. Those slates. It seems impossible now that they were ever countenanced. The squeak of the slate pencils and the peculiar and disgusting smell of the wood-framed slates still remain in the memory. The usual method of cleaning off one lot of work to make room for more was to spit on the slate and rub with the sleeve. Particular children did carry a slate rag, a shade more cleanly.

There was no paper work, and a famine scarcity of reading books. A sharp child learned a good deal in a limited fashion by memorising completely the little primer available. (In passing, how is it that we find so many old people who had only the drilling in the Three Rs of those bad old school days, better able to write a sensible letter, better spelt, than some of their grandchildren.)

I remember the last lesson one afternoon being left out for some good reason no doubt and I was sure that the teacher would suddenly remember and call the children back, I ran like the wind all the way home to get beyond the sound of recall. I recollect also being sent by the governess soon after assembly one morning, to the school gate to see if there were any latecomers in sight before she closed the register. I spied the head of John, the big six-year-old bully of the school, projecting round the corner of a nearby alleyway. John was evidently contemplating 'playing dubs' or truanting. Knowing the painful consequences of giving John away, I reported no one in sight to the governess.

Such are the beginnings of cowardice and the part of discretion in valour!

Another incident concerned the redoubtable John too. This time a dozen or 18 of the youngest children were sitting precariously on those long plain stools at reading lesson, nothing at the backs, and their little feet dangling far from the floor. There were three stools forming three sides of a square, with teacher in her chair on the fourth side. I remember watching John, on one of the stools, beginning to rock gently to and fro without teacher noticing. The rocking increased gradually, and those who noticed were frozen in horrible anticipation. Finally the stool went backwards, with a line of heels in the air and heads bumping on the floor amid a chorus of howls. John went, too. He must have thought the game cheap at the price.

Queer how such little events remain in the memory through so many tears and the more searing incidents of adult life. One more remains – of being brought out and rapped on the knuckles by a young teacher. Not that the rapping remains, but the fact that I never knew or ever learned, what I had done amiss. That rankles in a child. Those who may think it necessary to punish a small child, however slightly, should surely be very certain that no lasting sense of injustice is left behind. The millstones about the neck were better!

Portsmouth Grammar School, founded in 1732, is a venerable educational institution with its home in what was part of the Cambridge Barracks.

School days were a far cry from the enlightened times in which we live, as this picture of children in an unidentified Southsea classroom illustrates so vividly.

Mile End House School was situated in one of the beautiful old homes along Commercial Road at Mile End, and is recorded here in 1975 prior to the large-scale redevelopment of that part of the city.

Spice Island had its Heyday in the Eighteenth Century

(First published February 25, 1953)

The charm of Old Portsmouth still lies in its strong suggestions of other days – times more leisurely than these, more placid in some respects, more violent and more lawless in others.

Broad Street seems to belong to the days of Tom Bowling and sailing ships, grog shops and hornpipes. The sea end of it is like an ancient and wooden-legged sailor with a tarry pigtail and strange tales to tell to whoever would listen.

There in the open space with its foot in the water, the windows of the Star and Garter looked out in their brighter days and saw much of the naval history of England in the salt-water traffic of the harbour, and below them in the street the rough waterside life of the changing centuries.

Not so many years ago they looked out across the harbour to the old *St Vincent* off Haslar Creek, where boys were hardened into tough sailormen of the old sort. A little farther up the harbour, nobly afloat and apparently everlasting, the *Victory* rode in retirement. The Gosport ferry boats used to pass close to her on their ha'penny journey, giving a glimpse of her held by great chains in the tide. Even then it used to be said that she was held in a sort of cradle because of the weakness of her old timbers. The Star and Garter now lies a 'sheer hulk' like poor Tom Bowling. The original premises date from the reign of Queen Mary in the middle of the sixteenth century, when there was little on Spice Island but the Round Tower. Like other waterside houses it used to pay to the Portsmouth Corporation a number of fat capons yearly as a sort of ground rent. Even the George in High Street could not boast more distinguished connections with historic figures. Nelson, Howe, St Vincent all knew it and lodged there, and William IV, when Duke of Clarence, frequently occupied a room overlooking the harbour in the days when, as a naval officer, he was given a hiding by an indignant but unwitting waterman for drinking the latter's beer at an inn in Tower Street. Drinking another man's beer would seem to be the eighth deadly sin, and Spice Islanders were always blunt people.

It is said too, that even an exiled king, Louis Philippe, once lived at the Star and Garter, and Dickens, that lover of inns, and Thackeray knew it well. The ground-floor window nearest the sea was famous for its scratched initials and names on the glass, including Nelson's in the corner, hemmed in by those of Dot and Flora. Unknown Dot and Flora, like the great admiral, have gone the way of all flesh, but they stimulate the imagination. Among many other names was Lemmie Go, some bygone wit whose humour was preserved for posterity.

But the most touching tale told about the Star and Garter and its harbour view concerns a tragedy and mystery of the cold seas and ice of the Arctic. In 1845 Sir John Franklin sailed in command of a little fleet of three ships to seek the North-west Passage, between Atlantic and Pacific north of Canada, as others had done before without success. His ships were the *Erebus* and *Terror*, names immortalised by the two volcanic peeks in the Antarctic. With them went a small supply ship, even smaller than the others. Three years later they abandoned the ships in the terrible northern ice. This was known from ships' papers found many years later. No man returned. Lady Franklin used to come every year to the room at the Star and Garter which she and her husband had occupied, to be with her memories and to cherish a hope which was not fulfilled this side of the grave. She even purchased a steam yacht – the *Fox* – and went in search of her missing husband.

Earlier than this, the eighteenth century shows a very different page in the history of Spice Island. The French wars and the consequent shipping activity brought Broad Street to its heyday. It was outside King James's Gate, and so outside the town's restrictions. There were in the early part of the eighteenth century 41 drinking houses of various sorts in Broad Street alone, and there was nothing to stop them being open all day and all night. Chroniclers leave no doubt about the character of Spice Island in those days. Cockfighting, gambling, drinking and worse were common, and bull-baiting in the middle of Broad Street was a Shrove Tuesday treat.

The artist Rowlandson's well-known picture of Portsmouth Point, portraying the sea end of Broad Street and its people, leaves still less in doubt, even though allowance be made for over emphasis.

All that is happily gone and the present attractions of this part of the city are realised by some of Portsmouth's most appreciative citizens who have chosen to live there. To those with nose for the past, the place is always tinted with the colours of other days, just as an old house has something about it that a new one lacks.

Demolition commences on the old Star and Garter at Point in 1954, in its heyday home to many of our historic naval heroes.

The year is 1933 and the home of the famous marine artist Wyllie is seen here adjacent to the Round Tower.

The famous window from the Star and Garter is pictured with the signatures cut into the glass. Nelson's name is here, along with Dot and Flora and the strange Lemmie Go.

A view from the water provides a different perspective of Point, with the Still and West to the left of the picture.

The plaque on the wall indicates Lord Howe's house in Lombard Street, Old Portsmouth.

Barrack Street, now rechristened with its original name of Peacock Lane, was another of the tiny streets of Old Portsmouth with a long pedigree.

Concern about the state of the Victory *was brought to a head when the battleship HMS* Neptune *rammed her on 23 October 1903, as can be seen in this rare picture. The* Neptune *broke loose from her two tugs as she was leaving harbour on her way to Germany after being sold to a German company.*

High Street, Old Portsmouth, boasted some beautiful buildings, although many were sadly lost in the war.

Memories of the Old Wooden Walls in the Dockyard

(First published 27 March 1953)

From all accounts it is not easy to stroll through the gates of the dockyard with small pretence to official business.

Back in the 1890s, as a small boy I used to find it easy enough to get in, and to feast my young eyes on ships and all that pertained to ships. It happened that I knew another, bigger boy who wore the blue smock of a butcher boy, and carried a big basket on his arm. He was not so very much bigger, and these days would still be at school. This butcher boy was sometimes sent with a loaded basket to deliver to a mess aboard the old *Marlborough*, one of the wooden walls that used to lie alongside the dockyard as a depot ship. I was glad to go with the bigger boy and see the sights.

I was not sure if I was supposed by the police on the gate to be a diminutive assistant meat porter. I hoped, being small, not to be noticed. Anyway, I was never turned back, but was always a bit nervous of the big policeman until the two of us were well past him.

Once in, we staggered on with the heavy basket, past where at least one of us knew they hanged Jack the Painter from the high mizzen-mast, long ago. We went on across the uncomfortable cobbles that I always remembered as a feature of the dockyard.

I cannot recall the exact spot where the *Marlborough* lay, but it seemed a good walk with much to see on the way, across railway lines and wire hawsers, by the side of deep docks and the edges of basins. Not far from the *Marlborough* was the old *Sultan*, one of those early ironclads, which was a sort of sail and steam hybrid. The *Vernon* and the *Victory*, too, were then floating ships and not shore establishments.

Arriving at the *Marlborough* we boys used to cross the big gangway and go down to the mess decks. Usually there were sailors there at a meal – the old-time sailors who made the Navy their life

for twenty-one years or more. We were invited to sit down at one of the clean, bare tables, and given a drink of tea. Not a cup of tea, but tea in a basin big enough for me, just a little fellow, to wash my hands in.

All this, the tea, the bare well-scrubbed tables, the timbers of the old ship, the rope yarn ship smell, and the friendliness of the sailors to a couple of youngsters, are well remembered, although Navy rations then did not allow much hospitality.

These sailors were of the period when training still included knowledge of sail, and many of them had graduated from Greenwich through the old *St Vincent* to the Navy. Some of them had seen service in the Victorian wars – little wars by comparison with those to come twenty years later – campaigns in Egypt, in Ashanti and in Burma, and little excitements like the chasing of slave traders off the African coast.

My father was one of those Victorian sailors who was one of those landed on the west coast of Africa in about 1872 to swell Sir Garnet Wolseley's force of soldiers that cut and fought its way through the bush to Ashanti, to teach the natives that human sacrifice was frowned upon by Her Majesty's Government. He brought away a permanent reminder of that journey in the shape of a scar on his head from a knobkerrie, when a sudden attack came as the force was settling for the night in the thick jungle. I remember seeing the medal issued for that campaign, one side giving in bas-relief a picture of the troops struggling through the thick bush, the other bearing the Queen's head.

These memories lead to some realisation of what the Empire owed to the Royal Navy and to the dockyard behind it, in those far off days. Let us be proud of the old-time sailors and soldiers of Victoria's day, who like their sons and grandsons 'did their bit'.

As a boy Richard Esmond went aboard the old wooden wall HMS Marlborough, *which was part of the Vernon establishment along with HMS* Warrior. *The* Marlborough *was being towed away to be scrapped in 1924 when she broke away from her tugs during a storm and sank in the Channel.*

Old and older! Southsea photographer Stephen Cribb captured the airship Parseval *passing over* HMS Victory *in Portsmouth harbour.*

The magnificent sight of HMS Duke of Wellington *dominates this harbour scene from 1890. One of the Indian troopships is alongside at the South Railway Jetty, and in the foreground are two of the hulks used originally as convict ships and then later as stores vessels.*

A quiet time for shipping activity at the entrance to the harbour.

The might of the Royal Navy is displayed during inspection time at Portsmouth in the tough days of Victoria's seaborne might.

The Prince of Wales – later Edward VIII – receives his first naval salute as a cadet as he goes aboard ship to cross to Osborne College.

The old Implacable *looks in a sorry state in harbour prior to being towed away. At the time she was the oldest warship afloat. On 2 December 1949 she was scuttled in the Channel, a decision described by many conservationists as 'a despicable act of vandalism'. A bugler played the Last Post as the explosives were detonated and she went to the bottom.*

The training ship Foudroyant *was a familiar sight in the harbour until 1987 when she was taken to her new home at Hartlepool, where she reverted to her original name of* Trincomalee.

The Foudroyant *is moored in the background of this busy scene. The passengers aboard the Gosport ferry doing harbour cruise duty would have had the opportunity to see the old wooden vessel close up.*

Portsmouth Dockyard and its Growth

(First published 16 May 1953)

'Round the walls' is a phrase to one remembering his Bible which might suggest trumpets and the seven circuits of the walls of Jericho. It once meant days of childhood and a quiet spot for play and games by the dockyard walls.

A walk around the whole extent of those walls, taken with an interested eye and a jogging memory, gives glimpses of more than just a wall. It tells a good deal about the dockyard and its growth.

It is quite a walk from the main gate at the Hard to Flathouse creek. Visitors, when they queue under the old wall at the main gate for Navy Days or to visit the *Victory*, may see the plaque above the little entrance. It says, under the monogram of Queen Anne: 'This wall was begun the 4th June and finished ye 13th December 1711.' This was not by any means the first enclosure of the dockyard, for walls of sorts are known to have enclosed the docks – then much smaller in area – since the time of Magna Carta. Although there seems to be some doubt whether the site of the earliest docks was not in fact where the Gunwharf stands, and where the creek leading in to the old millpond made a good muddy bed for ships.

However, 'this wall' in the inscription means the solid brick erection, varying from 12 to 20 feet in height, which runs from the Hard along Admiralty Road round many angles to the old Marlborough Gate near Bonfire Corner. Thereabouts it ended, and indicates the size of the dockyard in 1711, when Sir Winston Churchill's great ancestor, the first duke, was at the height of his fame and his name was used for the gate. This part of the wall has lasted for two and a half centuries, and is still good enough to act as the outer wall of the buildings inside.

Past the Marlborough Gate, the Queen Anne wall went on for a little way. Then later came the old prison, Trinity Church, and the old Anchor Gate. This small district is sadly unlike what it was. The little eighteenth-century houses and streets have given way to characterless blocks of flats and areas of concrete. The latter may have their points but they are hardly picturesque or lovable.

In the 1840s the dockyard was extended a little over a vanished part of Old Portsea, which seems to have been self-contained and self-sufficient enough to run its own concerns and every year elect its own mock mayor.

Along that high black wall used to come gangs of convicts from the prison down Anchor Gate Lane, in their broad-arrowed clothes and guarded by warders. They worked in silence tidying up the road.

The convicts from this prison, whatever the misdeeds that brought them there, have left their mark – a worthy mark – on Portsmouth, which should help to balance things for them. They did much of the building of Victoria Barracks, the making of Clarence Esplanade, and the levelling of Southsea Common.

The dockyard has been pushed out a little to include old Trinity Church and those tarred timber walls, but one can resume the walk along the wall opposite the naval barracks. Here is a wall of quite a different type – stone and brick of about 18 feet in height. It runs the whole remaining distance past Unicorn Gate up to the Royal Hospital, where it turns left for a straight stretch along Flathouse Road. There it turns inward just short of the quay and along to the tower by the water at the edge of Flathouse creek.

This wall was built in the 1860s and 1870s to include the big extension of the dockyard of those times. It too was the work of the convicts. At intervals, and especially at turns in the wall, are those familiar curved and loop-holed turrets, embrasures, or barbicans.

As a small boy walking by the wall with my father in the early 1890s I asked what the funny bumps on the wall were for. I was told that up there the warders sat to keep an eye on the convicts at their work in case they tried to escape. My father must have remembered the wall being built. It seems however to the modern mind rather an expensive and permanent device for keeping watch, when a temporary staging would seem adequate for such a duty. Maybe they were planned anyway as an embellishment of an otherwise long and unbroken length of wall, and were put to the use described by my father as well. Materials were cheaper then and certainly the labour was!

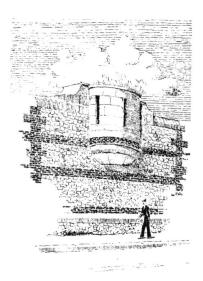

Richard Esmond drew this sketch of one of the 'funny bumps' in the dockyard wall.

A break in the dockyard wall allows workers to leave through the Pitt Street Gate, which was opened in the 1930s to relieve the pressure on the roads around the main gate and the Marlborough Gate.

The main gate was opened to allow Japanese sailors to march out to the cheers of townspeople and veterans of the Crimea in June, 1906, when the battleships Katori and Kashima visited the city. The Japanese, under Admiral Togo, had defeated the Russian fleet in May of the previous year, and the sailors were given the nickname of Togo's Heroes by Portmuthians.

The Japanese sailors are pictured leaving the Hippodrome Theatre after experiencing some traditional British entertainment.

In February 1919 a squadron of Japanese ships again visited Portsmouth, and officers and men were given the freedom of the tramway system while in port.

FREE PASS FOR PORTSMOUTH TRAMCARS.

VISIT OF
HIS IMPERIAL JAPANESE
MAJESTY'S SHIP,
"IKOMA,"
TO PORTSMOUTH.

The Mayor hopes that the Officers and Men of His Imperial Japanese Majesty's Ship, "Ikoma," will make full use of the Trams during their stay in this Port.

A busy corner of the dockyard in the 1940s is recorded here with HMS Vanguard in the background and HMS Sirius in the foreground.

Prisoners helped to build Clarence Esplanade at Southsea.

Were Portsdown Forts Lord Palmerston's Folly?

(First published 29 June 1953)

Strangers often ask questions about the forts in the sea at Spithead, wondering to see such structures rising out of apparently deep water. They are curious too about the hill forts on Portsdown.

Both are parts of the scheme of outer defences of Portsmouth, begun about ninety years ago, when the great Lord Palmerston was Prime Minister. The whole plan has been referred to as 'Palmerston's Folly' but it hardly seems folly to ring round the great naval and dockyard centre with defences that were up to date then, whatever they are now. Southsea was growing up, and the well-known shopping centre, though at first a residential road, was named after the same statesman. The Spithead forts – Spitbank the nearest and smallest, Horse Sand farthest east and No Man's Land nearest the island – are all built in shallow waters to command the deep-water channels, the only pathways for big ships. At low tide the sea bottom around the forts may be seen from a boat.

The three forts were begun in 1862 and built from blocks of granite with heavy oak timbers inside. Each has its own fresh water supply from

wells which pierce the seabed down to the under-lying clay. Spit Fort cost £165,000 to build, Horse Sand £424,000 and No Man's Land £462,000. The Portsmouth Town Hall, now the Guildhall, built about thirty years later, cost very much less than either of the two larger forts.

Spit Fort is built on the tip of the Spit Bank, which spreads from the Haslar shore out to this point, making shallow water all the way. Travellers on the Isle of Wight ferries will notice that at high tide their boat may cross the Spit Bank inside the fort, but at low tide passengers get a longer ride, for the vessel has to pass outside or east of the fort to make the deep-water channel. The two other forts, more distant, are less familiar from the Southsea viewpoint. They are seen merely as two silhouettes. Whether these sea forts are obsolete or not, they played a useful part in the defence of the port in both great wars. They mounted guns and searchlights, which were at times manned by local Territorials.

The forts on Portsdown must surely be fine places at which to be stationed if you are a fresh-air lover.

These forts date from the same time as those at

Spithead. From east to west they are forts Purbrook, Widley, Southwick, Nelson (near the monument) and Wallington. The cost of building them was about £100,000 each. Each looks north with a glacis of grassed earthworks, and from this side as was intended little of them could be seen.

The southern brick walls and gateways look over the Portsmouth they were built to defend. The views all round the compass are superb – across the Hampshire woods and pastures north to Butser, east to Chichester spire, south over Portsmouth, the Isle of Wight and Portchester, and west to the gleam of Southampton water and the green line of the New Forest, but happily the hill forts have never had to prove their worth in the manner for which they were built.

Troops manned the forts during the Second World War, and this picture shows stores being loaded aboard one by winch.

No Man's Land Fort never fired a shot in anger despite its prime position in the Solent.

When Fort Widley was built the old Widley windmill was lost to the Portsmouth skyline.

The Portsdown forts are still a distinctive feature of the Portsmouth panorama. In this 1930s shot the photographer has ventured inside Fort Purbrook.

Memories of Leigh Park Sixty Years Ago

(First published 3 July 1953)

'The stately homes of England, how beautiful they stand.'

One of the 'stately homes' set in its quiet parkland has now been converted into a council housing estate! To those who can look back far enough, there is a feeling of something precious and beautiful that has gone, or going, from the changing face of England.

Mrs Heman's well-known lines have been quoted time and again, sometimes sincerely, sometimes with bitter consciousness of the very many other homes of England that none could call stately or beautiful. That, one supposes, must be the justification for these great changes.

These thoughts came recently during a ride from Rowlands Castle to Havant by the side of Leigh Park. The wide parkland with its clumps of elm, once lovely and peaceful and green, is now a tumbled wounded mass; the never-before-disturbed undersoil thrown up in heaps from the gashes of trenches dug for drainage and foundations.

Back came summer days at Leigh Park sixty years ago, and the old-style Sunday school outing. For Portsmouth children this meant, most often, a day at Leigh Park.

Outing was literally the word. It is hard to express what a day in the green open country meant then to children shut in for the greater part of the year in town streets. Getting about then was not nearly so easy, and Leigh Park was then in the country. We owed a debt of gratitude to Sir Frederick FitzWygram, when Leigh Park was one of the stately homes with ever-open gates for so many of such outings. The ticket for those excursions used to cost sixpence, and that covered the return journey, usually by train, sometimes by horse brake, and a substantial tea. Those teas! They were laid on trestle tables on the grass near the little pavilion. Crowds of youngsters in their 'stiff' best clothing, with excited heated faces, swigged endless cups of tea, and shouted untruthful claims as to how many they had consumed. They broke all the rules about bread and butter before cake (it was butter!) and no 'pocketing' for later consumption. All in the open sunshine and the odour of trampled grass.

When the journey was by train, there was a long walk to the gate at the corner of the park. Then a gathering, an impatient one, round a tree near the gate, for a prayer by the vicar – usually the Rev. Lindsay Young of St John's – followed by happy release for all, and with a wild whoop all were free for the day in unlimited green grass and among shady trees. The long day over, the returning crocodile to the station was always quieter, but very happy and very tired. It was bedecked with bunches of roses for mother at home, bought at the cottages near the gate with pence carefully reserved all day for that purpose. To this day the scent of old-fashioned roses calls up in at least one memory of Leigh Park long ago.

Detraining at Portsmouth Town Station, two feelings were uppermost. One was of being nearly asleep with fresh air and the day's excitement, the other the almost hopeless realisation that for the next outing we had to wait for a whole year! And how nearly infinite is a year at that age.

The journey by horse brake was even more exciting. How lucky were those bigger boys and girls allowed to sit beside the driver at such a giddy height above the horses' backs. What a strange shape horses looked from there, and how tightly one clung with feet dangling, riding the bumps in the road and hoping the horses wouldn't bolt.

There was always a halt on the way back. Drayton then was a few houses and the inn. A Sunday school outing stopping at a pub seemed vaguely improper, but the horses had to be watered. What the drivers did round at the back when returning the buckets was not visible to us.

I once experienced a journey even more wonderful than the ride on the brakes. On the occasion of one outing I was taken in a horse van in the very early morning. The van was the advance guard carrying crockery and food to Leigh Park. My big brother was one of the helpers and under his mantle I was a VIP.

To sit by the driver on a folded sack, and sometimes to take the reins; to amble slowly all the way to Leigh Park along the country roads early in the morning was bliss. Particularly remembered over the years between is one bit of the journey – the open stretch between Farlington Church and Bedhampton Hill, with Portsmouth on the left and the long downward slope to Farlington Marshes and the sea forward and right. There on that then quiet and empty road, on that perfect summer morning, my young self experienced a sudden wave of feeling a sort of joyous appreciation of clean sky and sunshine, hedges, fields and sea, such as I never forgot.

Leigh Park House in the days when it was a stately home and the grounds were the venue for many a Sunday school outing.

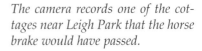

The camera records one of the cottages near Leigh Park that the horse brake would have passed.

By the 1950s the first homes were built to house the huge overspill of people from Portsmouth, many of whom had lost their homes in the blitz.

The Journey was Important Too

(First published 11 July 1953)

It was an old one-horse wagonette, seen in a Portsmouth street not long ago, piled high with junk wood for sale. A tumbledown anachronism, on its last legs or spokes, like a hobbyhorse at a motor show. The pony drawing it, even though its mouth may have told a tale, was much more youthful.

What tales that old wagonette might tell of pre-motoring days. It brought back the sharply-felt pleasures of those times, infrequent, but the more thoroughly enjoyed and clearly remembered. It was a wagonette like that which a family or two would engage for the day, paintwork bright and wheels sound, to drive, say, to Warsash with a crab tea in the offing.

When the great day came nobody hurried, particularly the horse. He seemed to know that wayside inns were natural stopping places. Possibly he numbered among his ancestors some galloping steed that knew the open door, the bustle and the refreshment of the coaching inns.

After rousing the echoes under the Hilsea arches with the easy clip-clop of his shoes, the Old Swan at Cosham gave him his first hope of rest. There a left turn into the Portchester Road led him before long through Wymering and on to Paulsgrove, where the pub by the water stopped him. This is not to say that such outings were old sagas punctuated by pubs. Out of the inn would come the old china mugs for the refreshment of passengers. It was said that now and again not all the mugs were returned, even empty. Let us suppose, kindly, that they were regarded as souvenirs of a happy day!

They used to tell us that Paulsgrove was so named because the Apostle landed there on his supposed visit to England. One wonders if he did, or if some lesser Paul gave the place his name, and the name suggested the tradition. Nearby Wymering Church, by the way, is the Church of Saints Peter and Paul.

On would go the wagonette by the Portchester crossroads and through Fareham's street of ample width, and out along the quiet dusty roads at a jog trot or a walk. The pace certainly allowed the company to see and enjoy everything.

Warsash by the quiet water was reached eventually, although sometimes trifles such as the parting of a leather strap or trace, or the loosening of a hubcap, caused fluster and delay. I remember little of Warsash over the years except a row of cottages on the right facing the water; the little cottage parlour in which we ate the famous crab tea; and a stroll down to the little lagoons of shallow water in which the captive crabs were kept as in condemned cells, until they were taken out to meet their gastronomic fate. That was Warsash at the turn of the century, and I have not partaken of a Warsash crab since.

There was something Dickensian about those Victorian family jaunts in the warmth, the intimacy, the lack of hurry, the roads and the welcoming inns. One did not merely go to Warsash or some such place; one journeyed to Warsash, and the journeying was as important and as enjoyable as the arriving. Interest and incident marked the way, as it did for the Pickwickians. It was the sort of thing that illustrates the difference between those placid days and these of the jet age.

I remember as a small boy, being lifted up for a ride on the saddle of a penny-farthing bike by a cousin from Chichester who, perched aloft, had dared to ride the long adventurous 18 miles on dusty bumpy roads and solid tyres, to get to Portsmouth. Today that journey is a mere half-hour trip by car.

To arrive seems to be all, but much may be missed on the way. What would grandfather think about it, and if inanimate things could muse on life, what would the old wagonette mutter to itself on the junk round? It has not 'arrived' even yet at the end of its long journey, but it has been useful and seen some fun on the way. Not a bad epitaph!

This charming picture was taken on Easter Monday 1899 and eloquently depicts the slower pace of life at the end of the nineteenth century.

The main road at Portchester takes on a surreal character as this unusual aerial view shows. Barges are moored at the old oil depot.

Little-Used Pathways on Portsdown Hill

(First published 8 October 1953)

Imagine if you can Portsdown Hill levelled, and the countryside inland from Portsmouth as flat as the city itself; with neither of those two wonderful views from the hill – south over the city and north over south Hants – to please the eye. Then be grateful for the geological quirk that gave us the hill.

The geologists tell us that the hill is the result of a few million years' work by the tiny marine creatures whose remains form the chalk of the hill. But there was surely some little cherub aloft with a benevolent eye on the city that would one day sit at the foot of the hill, who had a hand in it. To him our thanks.

A little way up the steep hill road opposite the George there was a break in the hedge where a path led downward by the new reservoir. I used

to be able to stand there and admire the rolling country up to Butser. Now the reservoir makes necessary a short walk down the path to uncover that view. This byway runs parallel with the London road to Purbrook. Years ago you could imagine yourself far from any main road, but now for a good way the gardens of the houses on the western side of London Road run down to it. Yet is is still very quiet and makes an attractive alternative to the busy main road.

On one of those October days stolen from summer it proved an enjoyable walk. True, the grass underfoot was still wet from the morning mist, there were overhanging bramble sprays to be avoided, and the long autumnal strands of spiders' webs made feeble barriers across the way. About a mile down, the path turns sharp left along the hedge where a field of greens bars the way. Then it dips into a little tunnel of undergrowth and trees before it turns right again to resume its original direction north.

Here on the far side to the tunnel the blackberries were thicker than one had ever seen them. No searching would be necessary; a pie of family size could be furnished without moving a yard. On the other side of the path a field of golden stubble sloped up to meet the clean blue sky. The keen flavour of the berries in the mouth, and the delight to the eye of the autumn blue and gold seemed complementary, like nuts and wine or bacon and eggs.

Farther on came a little bridge and running under it the little brook of Purbrook after it had left the village away on the right. Here it was on its way to Southwick and the Wallington stream that reached salt water at Fareham.

It was not easy here in rural quiet to remember that the traffic was rolling and roaring only a couple of fields away. To the west of the main road it is peaceful, for the new Purbrook has grown up almost wholly to the east. The path now came out on a metalled road at Purbrook Heath, with its one or two pretty old houses. But at the point where the path met the roadway something curious appeared to the inquisitive eye. Going back towards Portsdown was the beginning of what looked like a sunken grassed-over roadway.

It was later in the walk, during a chat with a pleasant young man who was clearing a hedge, that it appeared that the old roadway is thought to be a Roman road, coming from Portsdown and on northwards. Ploughmen on its course have at times been held up by Roman road building thoroughness. How often ploughmen, more than most people, turn up the past in their scratching at the face of old England.

On emerging from Purbrook Heath a right turn takes one to the bridge at Purbrook. A left turn, however, leads away from the village past Southwick House. A signpost below had said: 'Potwell one mile'. I had to admit that I had never

before come across the name. Potwell is still in the future for me, for I was seeking the site of old Widley Church and the road branched left before Potwell appeared.

The narrow deserted and meandering road from here to the site of the old church crosses the brook lower down its course. It is a fact that in spite of busy congested roads, one can in a matter of minutes reach quiet byways and where one might be in another century. This is particularly true of the area just 'over the hill' between Purbrook and Fareham. This little road to Widley indicates by its serpentine progress that it is a very ancient way, that grew out of tracks trodden by men's feet across the dry spots of the valley when much of it was marshy and wooded.

The site of old Widley Church proved to be only a site now – churchyard walls and tombstones lying flat and at peace undisturbed. Above on the hill the green bank of Fort Widley looked down. The quiet was broken only by the sound of cows in the nearby farmyard.

Back then all the way to Purbrook. The village like many others, which bestride main roads, has suffered from the necessity of road widening. Bypasses have, among other virtues, that of leaving an old village to sleep in peace. That easy part is not for Purbrook. The village used to be little but the one rising street on the main road. It is ancient enough, but was never a separate parish until 1831. It was merely a part of the large and historic parish of Farlington. The Church of St John was built soon after, and is therefore, although its builders followed the traditions of the village church, not old enough to attract the hardened antiquarian.

The bridge over the brook at the foot of the street shows a stone inset which says it was widened in 1791. Nelson from his coach on his way to Portsmouth might have seen that being done. By now a rather tired lover of byways was more sensible of the advantages of straight main roads and exhaust fumes given off by south-bound buses. Highways and byways – one wants it both ways!

Thatched cottages at Southwick recall a simpler and slower pace of life.

The London Road at Purbrook in the quiet days between the wars, with Purbrook Church on the right of the picture.

The George Inn at the summit of Portsdown Hill recalled on a sunny day when a stroll needed a parasol and a walking stick.

One of the picturesque old cottages at Purbrook Heath that would have been seen by Richard Esmond while on his walk.

Widley Church was situated in a beautiful part of southern Hampshire. The church was built in 1850 on a site previously occupied by a much earlier place of worship. In 1950 the bell and the roof were removed, and by January 1953 the entire church had been demolished.

Only the overgrown outline of the church walls and some of the gravestones recall the old Widley Church. The site can still be seen today.

Was the Old Southsea Line Abandoned Too Soon?

(First published 10 November 1953)

There are two straight scars on the face of Portsea Island, scars still easily traceable. They cross each other near Fratton station.

One is the line of the old canal; the other the path of what was Southsea's own railway. These lines are the only reminder of two unsuccessful enterprises. Incidentally they dictated the layout of the streets that came later along their courses.

In the 1850s Southsea was becoming a place in its own right. Residents thought a railway, which would link Fratton to a point near the seafront, should serve it. In 1867 parliamentary sanction was given through a Private Member's Bill for such a line. Local promoters hoped that with this permission granted, the companies serving Portsmouth – the London, Brighton and South Coast Railway and the London and South-Western Railway – would undertake the work.

Time went on and the companies fought shy of the idea. Finally the line of somewhere between one and two miles' length was built by local enterprise, and was formally opened in July 1885 by Lady Willis. Later it was taken over by the companies. It never became a paying success and was closed down finally between the two wars. The bridges were levelled and the track bought by a well-known local firm of builders. Some people thought at that time that it was an opportunity for the town to take it over, and many schemes were suggested for its use. One was to turn the track into a tree-lined walk for public use. The opportunity was missed, however. The line with its four necessary bridges cost £55,000 to build, a sum which seems small enough nowadays.

Passengers could travel for a penny or two along the line between Fratton and Southsea stations, in carriages open like tramcars, pulled or pushed by a little engine. Tickets were first or third class, bought from the conductor. There were halts – hardly stations – at Highland Road bridge and Jessie Road bridge. Considering the increasing number of people, visitors and residents nowadays in the area, it would seem that what was once a failure might have been a success.

It is still possible to follow its course. Branching off from a platform at Fratton station, it crossed Goldsmith Avenue under its first bridge. The second was not far on – the Jessie Road bridge – which occupied with its grassy ramps the open space now called The Square at the western end of Devonshire Avenue.

From there the line made a straight way between the end walls of the gardens in Bath Road and St Augustine Road. That is rather like putting the cart before the horse, for it was the railway that governed the length and straightness of those two roads, built after the line itself. To get from a point half way along Bath Road to a similar part of St Augustine Road still needs a long walk, although the distance over the roofs as the crow flies is very short. The railway prevented crossroads from one to another.

The line then went under Highland Road bridge, now levelled, but still referred to as 'the bridge'. In the first days of the Gaiety Cinema there were steps down from the bridge to the door. Now the steps go up from the door to the levelled road. On the other side of the bridge the line continued along the school wall in a shallow cutting, exactly where cars drive into the Odeon car park. It is more correct here again to say that the school wall was built along the line of the railway, for the school came later than the line.

This part of Southsea in the early days of the railway was not by any means the built-up area that it is now. The Festing Hotel and Festing Road houses were still to come, and only two or three large residences stood in the Craneswater Park area. From Highland Road bridge to the end of the line at Southsea station in Granada Road, near The Strand, was only a short stretch. Along this length the building went on, some of the St Ronan's Road and Craneswater houses looking across the line. Here was the last of the four bridges, where Old Bridge Road reminds us of its position. Not many yards on came the station. The station site is still concerned with transport, for a well-known garage now occupies it. The station itself was a quiet one, of course, but a much more pleasant place than many railways stations, with an open space between it and the road. Southsea visitors struggling along with heavy suitcases to reach a crowded bus would find Southsea station, if it had survived, more than pleasant.

In the early days that corner of Southsea was very quiet, and parts were very lonely. My brother, who as a boy worked at Smith's bookstall on the station, told how it was his job to deliver the *Evening News* to a few big houses in the Craneswater Park area. Sixty years and more ago, the round at night was rather a frightening ordeal for a small boy, and he has admitted that on some dark and stormy nights, with wind and rain sweeping in from Spithead making a howling in the trees, the papers did not get delivered, and he was glad to scurry back to the lights of the station bookstall.

After the First World War the old East Southsea station was leased to various businesses, including a firm of motor engineers and a building contracting company.

Jessie Road bridge with the brick pillars giving way to steps down on to the platform of the halt.

The camera moves forward to March 1995 and the East Southsea station terminus is finally demolished to make way for new homes. Much of the stonework and ornate cast-iron work has been preserved for the future.

Later the tiny engines were replaced by steam railcars, thought to be some of the first in the country.

This aerial view of Southsea clearly shows the curved path of the rail line at the bottom right of the frame.

Memories of Old-Time Stage Shows in Portsmouth

(First published 15 December 1953)

'Lets pretend,' say the little girls at play, and they hang their long coats from their waists, and are grown-up ladies with trailing skirts – or the boys creep about with feathers and tomahawks, and are Red Indians. It is a far cry from that to playing Lady Macbeth or Hamlet. Nevertheless, all are outbreaks of that urge to play-act that is inherent in human beings.

Acting satisfies a deep human instinct, and gives scope for what is called in these days, self-expression. Even in the case of professionals, one would guess that they act for more reasons than making a living. In fact, the world of greasepaint has a fascination for most people, even though the great majority stay permanently on the house side of the footlights. In spite of the flood of ready-made acting supplied by films and radio, the live stage does not lack enthusiastic lovers. Highbrow or lowbrow, Shakespeare, Marlowe or Shaw, opera or ballet, or the most boisterous music hall show, all have their patrons, and Portsmouth can look back over the years on a truly 'mixed grill' which has been varied enough to suit all.

In the old days the houses of entertainment in the town gave plenty of choice. This was before the arrival of radio, and even the phonograph, as it was first called, was hardly more than a toy. Those who were lucky enough to be carried to their evening's pleasure arrived in a jingling hansom or a sedate growler.

The Theatre Royal was the home of all that was first class in the theatrical world. Henry Irving played Hamlet there, and Ellen Terry played Beatrice in *Much Ado about Nothing*. A little later came the day of Martin Harvey of the flashing eyes and the silver voice, in such plays as *The Only Way* and *The Breed of the Treshams*, and the handsome Wilson Barrett in *The Sign of the Cross*. It would be difficult to mention a great name of the theatre who has not featured on the Royal bills.

In Lake Road at that time was the local home of melodrama – the Princes Theatre, which was opened in 1869 originally as a circus. Here could be had to taste, ' blood and thunder', pathos, and tears and virtue triumphant in such plays as *East Lynne* and *The Face at the Window*. Here, the villain was always rich, swarthy in looks and completely black in soul, and somehow frequently named Sir Jasper. The hero was poor, handsome, brave and a complete Sir Galahad, and was usually named Jack. The heroine was always innocent, virtuous and beautiful, and had a way of being cast out of her home into the snow. Country cousins, being taken to the Princes, were supposed to so lose themselves in the drama, as to yell aloud a warning to the hero or heroine, when the villain offered them the drugged or poisoned cup.

The leading variety house then was the Empire in Edinburgh Road, which was opened in 1891, the Hippodrome not being built until a little later. This was a real old-time establishment, where one could watch the turns and be supplied with drinks by hurrying waiters. In those days certain quite young gentlemen out for an evening's devilment often visited the Empire. Attendants, popularly known as chuckers-out, had to be stalwart types, and it was no uncommon sight to see young gentlemen land suddenly and unwillingly in a heap on the pavement outside, their share of the entertainment ended. Or was it only beginning?

Still more of the old sort was the well-known Vento's Temple of Varieties in Lake Road. Here, audience and performers were on such close terms that frank remarks and criticisms were often past between floor and stage. It was correct to take fish and chips, oranges and nuts to eat, and sometimes to use as missiles. For just a few pence all had a grand free-and-easy time.

The opening of the Hippodrome almost opposite the Royal, and of the King's at Southsea, in the early years of the twentieth century, gave Portsmouth a still greater choice in the days when the cinema was almost unborn. The Kings opened to present the best plays to the public, but it has seen changes for it soon became a twice-nightly variety house and then a picture house. Among its remembered earliest programmes were *The Merry Widow* with Lily Elsie in the title role, Jose Collins and Harry Welchman in *The Maid of the Mountains*, Edmund Willard and Madge Macintosh in repertoire, *Monsieur Beaucaire* and *The Wandering Jew*. Among the celebrities were Harry Lauder and the Great Lafayette.

Delving still farther back, there were the shows at the Portland Hall in Kent Road. Marie Hall, the violinist, played there, and there was a strange show called Poole's Myrioama, which unrolled a sort of endless canvas, painted scenes which moved slowly across the stage to roll themselves up again on the other side.

There was West's *Our Navy* at the Cogswell-designed Victoria Hall, one of the first, if not the very first, moving pictures Portsmouth ever saw. Those mottled flickering pictures were seen in the infancy of what has become such an enormous business, when Hollywood just meant timber. The show naturally aroused great enthusiasm among Portsmouth audiences, despite the jerky movements and over-quick marching of the sailors on the screen.

There was another music hall called Freddy Fordham's in or near Station Street by the Town Station, where Fitzsimmons the boxer gave an exhibition and broke the punching ball from its moorings.

Finally, almost a legend of the stage in Portsmouth was the old Bluebell, still remembered but perhaps better forgotten. Mother of them all, beyond living memory, was the old Portsmouth Theatre, built in St Mary's Street – later called Highbury Street – and transferred eventually to High Street near Buckingham House on part of the site of the Cambridge Barracks. Kean and Kemble played there and later Dickens knew it. Readers of *Nicholas Nickleby* will remember his account of it.

The old Portsmouth Theatre that once stood in St Mary's Street.

Vento's Theatre in Lake Road later became a cinema and was known as the People's Palace. The building survived until 1980 after seeing service as Blundell's store.

The Princes Theatre was another of Lake Road's places of entertainment. It too became a cinema but was destroyed during the blitz.

The interior of the Princes Theatre showing the ornate decoration and stunning proscenium arch.

The Victoria Hall, built in 1885, was a popular place to see Alfred West's early exhibitions of moving pictures. The hall was leased by Arthur Andrews in 1900. The building remained a cinema until 1960 when it finally closed – the final film was Expresso Bongo *starring a youthful Cliff Richard.*

The Hippodrome was opened by music hall star Marie Tempest in May 1907, when she was mobbed by crowds as she arrived in her open tourer.

During the visit of the French fleet in 1905, Alfred West showed scenes of both English and French sailors and soldiers.

Under the Distinguished Patronage of
the Admiralty and the Army Council.

VICTORIA HALL, SOUTHSEA.

COMMENCING MONDAY (Bank Holiday),
At 3 and 8. Doors open 2.30 and 7.30.
OPEN HOUSE TO OUR FRENCH VISITORS
Twice Daily during their Visit.
ENTIRELY NEW PROGRAMME,
Magnificent Animatographs of Life in
OUR NAVY AND OUR ARMY.
Arranged by Alfred J. West F.R.G.S.

L'ENTENTE CORDIALE.
FESTIVITIES AT BREST. FRENCH BLUE-
JACKETS AT WORK AND AT PLAY.
Reception on the Massena and Luncheon on the
King Edward VII., etc., to be followed
with Scenes at Cowes and Portsmouth.
GRAND NAVAL & MILITARY PAGEANT
PAST AND PRESENT, &c., &c.

Reserved Seats, 2s. and 1s. 6d.; Unreserved,
1s.; Admission, 6d. Service Men in Uniform
half-price to 1s. 6d. and 1s. seats. Seats booked
at H. Austin Storry's, Palmerston-road.
For further particulars apply to A. J. West,
Anchorage, Southsea.

A policeman keeps a watchful eye on the queue waiting to go into the Hippodrome on a Saturday night.

The Hippodrome was another casualty of the war and its site was almost the last to be redeveloped, a task that was delayed a little longer on 12 October 1984, by the discovery of a huge unexploded bomb beneath the foundations.

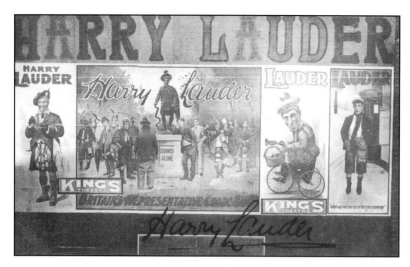

Harry Lauder was a frequent visitor to the King's Theatre. He autographed this card showing his posters decorating the outside wall of the King's.

Between 1913 and 1946 the Empire in Edinburgh Road changed its name to the Coliseum, changing back again following a post-war renovation. Charles Whittle, who was remembered for his song 'Let's all go down the Strand', signed this rare picture. He died in 1947 aged seventy-three.

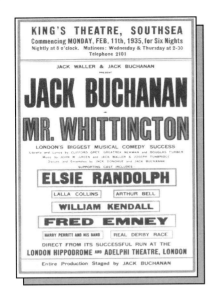

Matinee idol Jack Buchanan also appeared on the stage at the King's.

By the 1970s the city centre was being given a complete facelift, and this view shows how things have changed. The Theatre Royal takes centre stage, and in the foreground is the bus depot that used to stand in Hyde Park Road.

The Theatre Royal, pictured here in 1905, is still a working theatre today and, like the King's, brings the ambience of a bygone age to the world of entertainment.

When the Church Bells Called Beyond the Meadows

(First published 12 January 1954)

To walk across the quiet fields to the parish church hardly suggests this closely built-up area that is Portsmouth. Yet it could have referred to Portsmouth not so very long ago. My mother used to talk about the walk from Portsea to St Mary's, Kingston, in just that way, for the second half of the journey was along Church Path.

Most people know of Church Path as a passage between the backs of houses, although a few little dwellings were built facing it. It is difficult to imagine it as an ancient right of way across the meadows.

Eighty odd years ago the Portsea ramparts had then lately been demolished, and the Lion Gate across the end of Queen Street had just been taken down. Outside the gate the moat was filled in and the bridge was taken away. From there, Lion Gate Road, as Edinburgh Road was then called, ran across the open ground of the glacis and on up to Commercial Road. On the left outside the Lion Gate was the main gate of the Anglesea Barracks.

There was no Victoria Park on that open ground. The park was not opened until 1878 and was about the first open space, apart from Southsea Common, for public use in Portsmouth. It was then known as the People's Park. Neither was the Roman Catholic Cathedral a feature of the other side of Lion Gate Road. That was opened in 1882. Evidently our churchgoers' walk was very unlike the Edinburgh Road of today.

Where Edinburgh Road joins Commercial Road, Sunday pilgrims used to see the tall pillar erected to the memory of 'a gallant officer and true-hearted man in advancing the welfare of the British sailor.' It was paid for by the lower-deck shipmates of Admiral Sir Charles Napier and erected three years after his death. It was a remarkable tribute by the rank and file to an officer whose humanity and concern for those in his command were outstanding, especially in the days when the common sailors received more kicks than pence. Only the Nelson monument on the hill suggests itself as being anything like it, for each was built with the money freely given by the lower deck in honour of a beloved leader. The Napier column is now in Victoria Park.

Across the road from the Napier column was the beginning of Church Path. It ran beside the Bedford Hotel, often called then the Halfway House, being halfway between Portsea and Kingston Church. The Bedford was on the site of a very old inn called the Blacksmith's Arms. Here the field path to the church began, an old right of way dating at least from the earliest days of Portsea, and maybe very much before that.

The last part of Church Path became Church Road, and here we are close to its end and in sight of the church. Eighty years ago the church before us was not the present fine structure. It was a small, rather poor looking village church, built in 1843 but with a tower saved from a yet older building. The original church dated from the twelfth century and was a little older than old St Thomas's, the cathedral of today.

The present fine church dates from 1887 and we owe it largely to the generosity of W.H. Smith, afterwards Lord Hambledon, of the well-known firm of booksellers. Its tall tower is high but I have heard it said that a spire in addition was originally intended.

It says something for the growth of Portsmouth that within this period of eighty years, St Mary's changed from a small church over the meadows to it present fine establishment.

The earlier St Mary's was demolished to make way for the new building.

St Mary's Church stands at the end of what was a major path across the meadows. It cost a total of £47,000 and was opened on 9 August 1887, by the Empress Frederick of Germany.

Municipal 'White Elephant' Became a Profit Maker

(First published 12 August 1954)

A recent fire alarm at South Parade Pier inevitably reminded me of the fire that wrecked the old pier. The old pier was thought of with some affection, although it could not claim the looks or amenities of the present imposing structure. It was a typical Victorian pier with the usual cover at the entrance and a long open middle stretch with a pavilion at the sea end. It was privately owned and was opened in 1879 by Princess Edward of Saxe-Weimar, whose husband was then the Lieutenant Governor of the garrison. Waverley Road in Southsea used to be Saxe-Weimar Road until the First World War made German names unpopular. Southsea, almost unique as the seaside resort with strong naval and military connections, has from its beginnings owed much to prominent service personalities, from Lord Edward FitzClarence to high-ranking officers of the present day.

Present also on the occasion of the opening was one of the MPs for the borough – Sir James Elphinstone. He recalled then his memories of Southsea Common in the 1820s when it was a wasteland of gorse and swamps, and he found it necessary to take with him a bulldog and a thick stick when walking across it. It is on record that there were 'snipe in abundance' beyond Southsea Castle for the sportsman who ventured that far from Portsmouth in those days.

Southsea was a very much quieter place during the twenty-five years that the old pier gave service. But there were grand entertainments put on there, among them the old Musketeers concert party. Prices were usually sixpence and threepence, and the pier toll was tuppence.

All this came to a sudden end in 1904, for on 14 July fire wrecked the pier. Youngsters in school heard the news and neglected tea to rush out to see the still-smoking pavilion. Fortunately there were no casualties, a thing that could not be said about another Southsea fire in that first decade of the new century. The fire at the old Queen's Hotel claimed the lives of three maid-servants trapped on the upper floors. For some time the pier was derelict – black ruins and twisted metal – but in 1906 the corporation purchased the remains with the intention of building a new pier. The present handsome structure cost £70,000 and was opened in 1908 by the Mayor, Ferdinand Foster.

There was some difficulty about the sinking of the piles of the heavier structure, for it appears that the site occupied the mouth of an old creek or inlet possibly connected with Southsea's patch of bog-land which stretched across the Clarendon Road area. Incidentally another patch of low-lying and swampy land once occupied the site of the Albert Road police station, which was previously the public library.

So Southsea gained a very fine pier in addition to the Clarence and Victoria, both of which have their own stories. But it seemed that the Southsea of about fifty years ago was not ready or not busy enough for it. It did not pay its way, and became known as the municipal ' white elephant'.

For a time the new pier was given over to roller skating, a craze then much boosted by the American firms that made the skates. It was hardly enough to make the pier a success. Both large and small halls, as well as the outside deck around the bandstand, were open to skating. Even the balcony was available as a vantage point to watch the skating below. There was much fun for skilled skaters and beginners alike. It was remarkable what a shaking thud the latter made when they came down suddenly on the deck. As usual, sailors were enthusiasts, and seemed to make a speciality of backward skating; causing collisions and multiple upsets, which may possibly have been accidental.

Things soon changed for the pier and with the accelerated growth and popularity of Southsea as a resort it became a great attraction and the focal point of the seafront. The 'white elephant' has become a gilded pet, taking on its broad back some part of the city's financial burden.

By 1906 the Portsmouth Corporation had purchased the site and the construction of a brand-new pier was under way.

The old South Parade Pier was opened in 1879 but was destroyed by fire on 14 July 1904.

Workers travel out to the end of the pier on the makeshift cable transport.

The ornate frontage of the new pier – opened in 1908 – is impressive.

Pier attendants await customers when it cost just 2d to visit Southsea's newest attraction.

The Esplanade Hotel and part of Clarence Pier are visible in the background of this crowded Victorian beach scene.

Roller skating was an American craze that caught on in Great Britain, and Southsea's handsome new pier proved to be the ideal venue during the early years of the last century.

The bandstand at the end of the pier gave visitors the opportunity to listen to music and watch the passage of the ships in the Solent.

Clarence Pier was the brother of South Parade Pier and was also a popular meeting place for young and old.

A closer view of the bandstand shows its ornate cast-iron tracery and town crests.

The old Victoria Pier was situated past Clarence Pier near the Hot Walls.

When Langstone Led to Hayling Causeway

(First published 9 September 1954)

One of the luckier days of late August – a clear day of warm sunshine – seemed a good time to revisit the quiet area of Langstone Bridge. For apart from the constant traffic along the by-pass to the bridge and Hayling, this is a quiet spot. It seems to hold the sunshine and the warmth, and is surely a good place for gardens and farms.

To turn down South Street by the church in Havant takes one away from the east and west traffic along the Southampton-Portsmouth-Chichester road. That road has been a busy one since the Romans built it, or did they only improve what was already there? Roman roads are comparatively modern to some of the tracks that span England.

In quiet South Street, not far down on the right, is something to hold the eye in passing. It is an old half-timbered inn called the Old House at Home, which dates from Tudor times, maybe from the days of the other Elizabeth. Like the nearby church it has watched Havant from its days as a small market town busy with its tanneries and parchment making, to its present-day spread northwards over the domains of its squires. Though only in fiction, Conan Doyle's

Micah Clarke must have known the inn before he left home to fight in a lost cause.

These musings lasted as far as where the road is joined by the by-pass with its traffic for the bridge. Then the road is pleasantly tree-shaded. Beyond the level crossing over the single Hayling line is the turn left into the hamlet of Langstone, away from the traffic.

The road runs through the small village straight into the water, as Broad Street does at Point. When a spring tide and the right wind combine there is another likeness to Point, for the water comes well up the street.

Little Langstone has never been very big or very busy. It seems to have grown up at the ancient crossing point to Hayling. It is part of Havant parish, so boasts no church of its own. There were salterns there long ago, and some fishing, which has dwindled in amount. Oyster beds here, as at Hayling, used to be of some importance, and cockling is still done.

On the shore looking over at Hayling, good use is being made of old buildings by discerning people, who are turning them into waterside dwellings with views. On this particular sunny day there was less than a dozen people about – not enough to break the peace. Another fine old inn, the Royal Oak, probably dating from soon after the event that made the name so popular, stands on the sea wall only two or three yards from the shore. The inn was quiet, enjoying or enduring that afternoon siesta enforced by law, and looking as pubs do then, as though it were nodding, with eyes closed.

By the oaken seats against the inn wall were four or five young children with their mothers. The children were honey-coloured in swimsuits. Their costumes might have surprised the Royal Oak's customers of a century ago, but their physical condition and looks were tributes to modern methods of child rearing. On another seat was a gentleman looking bronzed, too, and very content in the sun, who had no objection to sharing his seat with me.

He was on holiday from the Midlands, but had lived and worked most of his life in Portsmouth, and was staying at Denvilles. He was charmed with his discovery of Langstone, and said that the grasses or weeds at our feet, uncovered at low tide, reminded him of the banks of the Tigris.

Some Langstone people have it that the weeds visible in the mud at low tide are not really of the sea, but originated from corn spilled in the days when the nearby mill was in use. Other local lore insists that the causeway running out towards Hayling is Roman. It is still very useful. Before the existence of a bridge a causeway did cross to

Hayling. The channel was anciently known as the Sweare Deep. The sea has encroached much during the centuries here and also over much of Hayling Island, and the crossing must have become difficult. The necessary parliamentary authority for building the bridge was given in 1823. The railway was later, of course. The old bridge has therefore served its term long enough, but plainly must make way for one adequate for modern needs, and without annoying and delaying toll payments.

With reference to past inroads by the sea on this part of the coast, it is on record that in the fourteenth century, particularly, there were great inundations. In that century the hamlet of East Stoke was completely submerged, and Hayling priory suffered great loss by the drowning of priory buildings. The flooding continued in after years, and to add to the misfortunes of the island, almost half its population died of the Black Death in that same period.

Round the corner past the Royal Oak are the picturesque old mill buildings. Both waterpower and wind power were used. The windmill has lost its sails now, and the buildings have been charmingly converted to a residence looking over Hayling and Chichester harbour, and enjoying all that sun and sea and salt air can give.

Here is a corner, for those who like such retreats, very near the summer traffic stream and within easy reach of the busy haunts of men, yet somehow suggesting the mood of 'the world forgetting, by the world forgot'.

West Street in Havant would have been Richard Esmond's starting point for his visit to Langstone. St Faith's Church is on the right, with South Street turning down next to it.

The interior of St Faith's pictured in 1934.

Havant was famous for its parchment where the special qualities of the Homewell spring produced parchment of the whitest quality. This is one of the lime pits pictured at a time when the trade was diminishing.

The Langstone foreshore is pictured before the last war with the Royal Oak public house in the far distance.

The old mill at Langstone is a familiar sight to all who cross into Hayling. It was built in about 1730 and was still at work in 1857.

The same area recorded in later days, and proving that 'messing about in boats' is a pastime which never seems to lose its appeal.

The old Langstone Bridge – opened in 1824 – and the railway line that carried the Hayling Billy and thousands of holidaymakers to the island, pictured by an intrepid aerial cameraman in the 1920s. The tollhouse for the bridge can be seen at the centre of the picture.

Some of the old cottages at Langstone are pictured in 1934.

Hayling Island has always been a popular holiday destination with its beaches and quaint area. This evocative picture shows West Town in the 1930s, with its signpost guiding anyone willing to walk to the beach.

The old bridge became inadequate for modern traffic because of its narrowness and weight restrictions. Bus passengers were often forced to walk over the bridge before letting the empty bus follow.

By 1956 the new bridge was built, running parallel to the older one until construction was finished.

There was always the ferry on hand for visitors from Portsmouth to return home.

Portsmouth's Civic Centres Through The Ages

(First published 21 April 1955)

Whatever the merits or demerits of Portsmouth Guildhall as architecture, there is no doubt at all as to its place in the affections of most Portsmouth people.

It is not coincidental that the Pompey Chimes are borrowed from it bells, that children in the days when the coalman with his horse and cart shouted his wares, imitated his cry with: 'Town 'All, Town 'All.' The Town Hall was the very centre of civic life and the building a source of pride to the people. Yet it is not an old building by any means, and it is interesting to look back on its predecessors in the little Portsmouth of long ago.

The earliest hint of local government in Portsmouth seems to be a reference to a King's Hall, a name connected with the upper end of Penny Street. As far back as William the Conqueror such halls were established for local government, although the government was hardly 'local' in the modern sense.

It is worth noticing how centres of local government in most parts of England came to be called Guildhalls. The guilds of medieval times were not directly concerned with local government. These trade guilds in the early-Middle Ages were associations of master men in their own trade.

Later, with the rise of the merchant princes who were businessmen rather than master craftsmen, the guilds were not such intimate concerns, and the gap between master and men widened. The guilds then became associations of 'big business' and it was the big men of business who

took a leading part in the affairs of the town. So the Guildhall meant local government in the end, and the old name persists.

Incidentally, now that Portsmouth has attained city status, there may be many who would wish the city fathers to consider naming the building City Hall, as a more correct and weighty name, and one that comes more easily off the tongue.

There used to stand in the middle of the road in High Street, Old Portsmouth, the first Portsmouth Town Hall. Traffic problems were not so acute then, and there was just room on each side of it for wagons, packhorses or coaches to pass. It is shown on old prints as the typical town meeting place, built on stilts as it were, with open market space on the ground floor. This building took the place of an earlier one on the same site. A well-off citizen of Portsmouth, named Carpenter, who was in his time mayor of the town, built this older one in Henry VIII's time. He built it as a town house but later it seems to have served as a municipal centre.

To revert to the later building of the eighteenth century, it still proved inadequate, and could not have been a pleasant meeting place, for in the middle of the street at one end of it were the local butchers' shambles. The building as it was then must have been familiar to Nelson and his men.

When the first municipal elections were held in Portsmouth on Boxing Day 1835, following the Municipal Reform Act, one of the first matters before the new council was the question of a new meeting place. On 24 May 1837, the year of Queen

Victoria's accession, the foundation stone of the building in High Street, known as the Guildhall, was laid.

The band of the Royal Marines was prominent at the ceremony, its members dressed in white plumes and scarlet trousers. It was opened in the following year on the day of Queen Victoria's coronation. It served for forty years and more until a growing Portsmouth felt the need of a building more central and more in keeping with its dignity. Meanwhile, the Guildhall in the High Street served as a museum, finally being destroyed in the war. To youngsters in its museum days it had rather a fearsome attraction. It was quiet and rather musty in the big room at the top of the stairs, which held many strange exhibits. Nelson pictures, letters and busts were most attractive, but most productive of shudders in the young was the dark brown desiccated finger of erstwhile dockyard arsonist Jack the Painter. His real name was John Hind and he was eventually hanged sky-high from the 64ft-high

mast of the *Arethusa*, and thereafter in chains at Blockhouse Point. The thumb had been used by some early owner with a gruesome sense of humour as a stopper to tamp down the hot tobacco in his pipe.

The planned new Town Hall was under discussion for some years until 1879 when the final go-ahead was given, but the foundation stone was not laid until another nine years later. At last the Prince and Princess of Wales, later Edward VII and Alexandra, opened the building familiar to all Portsmouth on August 9, 1890.

Although I was too young to remember, I have been assured that I was among the groups of people who made a tour of the £140,000 building after its opening.

Between the two wars, when Portsmouth became a city, the name was changed to that of the Guildhall. Although the magnificent building suffered during the blitz it is beginning to rise Phoenix-like from the ashes to become its former proud self.

The old Portsmouth Town Hall that used to stand in High Street and later proved to be inadequate.

With the building of the current Guildhall the older premises in High Street, Old Portsmouth, were converted into a museum. The building was destroyed in the war.

The new Guildhall was opened in 1890 on land that was originally owned by the Government.

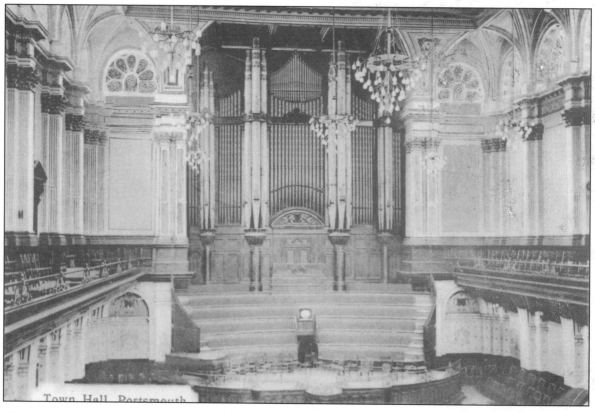

The great organ dominated the main hall of the Guildhall.

Architect William Hill of Leeds, who had previously designed the Town Hall at Bolton, seen here, designed the building. The similarity can be clearly seen in this postcard image.

The floodlights in this picture from 1934 enhance the splendid lines of the Guildhall.

Workmen pile sandbags around the Guildhall at the beginning of the war – a precaution that was taken for many other public buildings.

The Guildhall was all but destroyed by enemy action on 10 January 1941, and only the outer walls were left standing. By the early 1950s rebuilding work had commenced, clearing the rubble and paving the way for the beautiful building we all know today.

The Guildhall tower is swathed in scaffolding as the final stages of rebuilding takes place, in preparation for the official opening by the Queen on 8 June 1959.

An intrepid photographer secures an unusual view through the clock face looking out over the city towards the harbour.

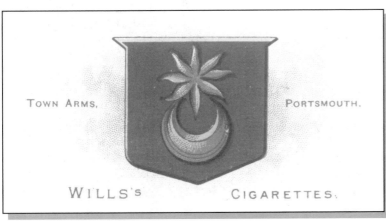

The Portsmouth town crest was featured in a popular set of cigarette cards issued by W.D. and H.O. Wills.

This Farlington Rent was a Pair of Spurs

(First published 21 October 1957)

One by one the ancient parishes or manors that lie around the fringe of the growing Portsmouth have been absorbed into the city area. Farlington is one of these, the church and three or four houses near it struggling like Wymering to keep a little oasis of rural England among the new growth of the past forty years or so.

Farlington Church used to stand almost alone, marking a stage along the road – the country road – from Cosham through a tiny Drayton to Havant and Chichester. The road was not lined each side then with houses; on the north side the land swept up to the top of Portsdown; to the south were the gently-sloping fields to Farlington marshes and the sea. The name of Farlington then meant little more than the marshes and a racecourse to Portsmouth people. To children, the church marked a step on the way to Leigh Park on a Sunday school outing by horse-brake.

Yet Farlington was for many centuries an important parish that stretched from the shores of Langstone Harbour up the Portsdown slopes, down the other side and away to Waterlooville.

Purbrook and Stakes, Portsdown and Drayton were all within its bounds. It was a strip of land measuring four miles north and south and about one-and-a-half miles wide.

It was certainly what is usually called a 'scattered' parish – not one of the more compact sort with a dozen or more houses clustered round the parish church. One wonders how much parish visiting was possible for a rector in bygone days, when a jogging pony was the only means of locomotion beyond walking, especially as that part of the parish north of Portsdown was wooded – part of the Forest of Bere. And not all the characters to be met in the woods were Robin Hoods.

The parish is much smaller now. Purbrook built its own church in Victoria's time, and Christ Church on the hill was built later in the same reign – in 1874.

It is a fact that despite general and age-long agreement that it is best to steer clear of the law, we would know very much less of what went on through the centuries were it not for lawsuits and records of ownership of lands.

The holding of land in return for loyalty and service to the overlord was of course the basis of the feudal system, and the records of changes and disputes connected with it are mines of information beyond the facts they chronicle. As long ago as 1187 there was a lawsuit concerning Farlington.

Later, in 1248, Roger de Marlay granted land and a yearly rent of seven shillings in Farlington to William, son of Alan Staker and his wife Ellen. William paid yearly for this, a pair of gilt spurs at Michaelmas to his overlord. The spurs of course were a sign of his obligation and fealty. The name of that thirteenth-century tenant is still very much alive 'over the Hill'. About eighty years later, in 1327, the manor was given to Alice, wife of Edmund, Earl of Arundel, for the support of herself and her two young sons. An ancient tomb on the north side of the nave of Chichester Cathedral supports the stone effigies of Richard, Earl of Arundel, with his wife by his side, dated 1346–97. Was this Richard perhaps the grandson of Alice of Farlington? The stone figures make a touching picture, for the wife's right hand is stretched across to be clasped in her husband's right hand, and in his left is held the gauntlet he has taken from the hand that clasps his wife's. One hopes that this reveals a story of true love six hundred years old and is not merely the sculptor's fancy.

But to return to Farlington – twenty years later the manor was in other hands, for it is recorded that in 1348 it was granted to the Priory of Southwick 'to mend losses through the invasion of the King's enemies.' The enemies were undoubtedly the French, who in those years of the Hundred Years War made many raids on the English coast. It was in 1338 that they landed at Portsmouth and burned the town.

People like the monks of Quarr in the Isle of Wight were building, in those years, a wall round their monastery to keep out the same raiders – a wall of which parts still remain. It is not surprising that Southwick Priory suffered, too.

At the Drayton end of Farlington parish, an interesting record shows that Lawrence de Pageham held lands in Drayton. In return it was his duty to supply a man in time of war to guard the east gate of Portchester Castle for fifteen days. This was in 1348, the year of the Battle of Crécy.

Farlington remained in the possession of Southwick Priory for nearly two hundred years, until the Dissolution of the Monasteries by Henry VIII in 1530 deprived the priory of all its belongings and even its existence. Farlington was then given to a William Pound, who must have been on the right side of Henry's fence. His family held the manor for well over a century.

In the nineteenth century it was in the hands of the Deverall family, a name still familiar in Farlington and the district.

The Church of St Andrew at Farlington is a new one as churches go, but is the fourth to be built on the same site. There was a church there in

1200, the earliest recorded date, but it may have been there long before. The present one was built in 1872–75. It boasts no extraordinary features, but it does incorporate in it some remains of the older buildings.

Out in the churchyard is the grave of one Luke Kent, who was a mail-coach guard. He left a sum of money to pay succeeding guards on the Chichester coach to sound their horns as the mail coach passed his grave. One supposes he had no other thought than that coaches would always be

the common means of transport, and that coach horns would continue to sound until the last trump.

Farlington has, or had, its ghost too before it was urbanised. Tales are told of a beautiful maiden on a farm who, like pussy, fell into a well and haunted the place thereafter. It fits in with the older quieter Farlington before buses and cars, when even on the main road the cry of the curlew on the marshes might be heard, and the oyster catcher and cormorant can be seen in flight.

Farlington Rectory in the 1930s takes a camera call. The building is still standing.

*Farlington's St Andrew's Church,
a flint building of great beauty.*

*The camera looks towards the
stained-glass window of Farlington
Church.*

Pleasant Home of a Happy Family

(First published 25 January 1967)

I had been talking to the members of my family during one of their visits to the 'old man' about some of my earliest memories of the family and of the Portsmouth that is no more. That last applies particularly to Portsea, where I was born long ago, when Portsea retained much of its separate character and eighteenth-century air when Lion Terrace and St George's Square were the homes of the sort of people who now live in newer parts, and the little streets were inhabited by naval and dockyard folk.

It needs an effort of the imagination and more verbal picturing than I can muster to show the Portsea of old. One must go back as far as Queen Anne to begin and forget the twentieth-century steel and concrete that has supplanted the mainly two-centuries old township.

No buses or coaches or even cars or bicycles carried the 'out-muster' home. Shanks's pony was all. Old Portsmouth was not near enough and was full anyway, and there were no commuters.

Running at right angles from Queen Street towards the then new dockyard wall were two streets – Cross Street and North Street. Between the two latter there grew up in the eighteenth century Prince George Street, King Street, Cumberland Street, Unicorn Street and Orange Street like rungs of a ladder of which North Street and Cross Street were the uprights.

It was in a tiny house in Orange Street, the most southerly of these, in which I was born in January 1887, and spent the first nine or ten years of my life. Tall flats set in acres of concrete now obliterate the street, and only one or two bits of kerbstone hint at even the direction of the street. My last glimpse of Orange Street as it was, was in the 1920s. I was back for a time in Portsmouth and wandered down that way for old time's sake.

I found that the side of the street on which my old home had been was a mass of rubble. Nothing of the old house was left upright, but as I peered closely at the spot I saw, bravely thrusting up out of the rubble, the old lilac tree of my childhood. Back came those immortal lines: 'I remember, I remember the house where I was born.'

The front door was entered directly from the pavement, and opened on a passage, one side of which was panelled in wood, separating it from the front room. Behind the front room was the sitting room, and behind that a stone-flagged kitchen with a big copper. This copper at the right season boiled the Christmas pudding for long hours; apart from its more frequent and prosaic use. The garden beyond was graced in the corner by the well-remembered lilac tree, but apart from that boasted little of flowers, being a playground for our youngsters. At one time when I was very small there were a few rabbit hutches in there, and somewhat later a few hens ran around.

At the house end of the garden were brick steps leading down to the cellar, which extended in two compartments under the rooms of the house. In the nearer part my mother did the family washing. That washing meant hard work. A washboard was used to rub the washing on, and the soap – called Watson's – came in pound bars, divisible halfway. No easy washing powders.

A thing I still hate to remember was the sight of my mother's poor hands on washing day, hands white and shrunken and wrinkled from long immersion in the soapy water. How often one wishes that it were possible to take back into the past the benefits of the present easier days and conditions for the dear ones of long ago.

The cellar served another purpose. It was our bathroom. The same big wooden tub, which was used for the washing, served for a bath for at least the boys of the family. I remember at four years of age sitting in that tub covered with lather, yelling my hardest because there was soap in my eye.

A small opening at the base of the wall in the street under the front window enabled the coalman to shoot the coal down. The opening under the front window was covered normally by a wooden flap that sloped at an angle of 45 degrees against the wall. I remember one frosty morning going to school with my brother, a couple of years my senior. All the way along the street I was making little runs up these sloping cellar flaps, and sliding back again. On one of them my feet slipped on the frosty surface and my chin came down on the window sill. On that window sill, as on most, was a small iron projection put there to lock closed shutters, and my chin came strongly down on it with gory results.

I got little sympathy from my brother, who assured me that now when I ate bread and jam it would leak out of the hole. I fancy I can still feel that little scar.

To stay for a moment with the puddings at Christmas, ours were home-made in a huge and deep earthenware vessel, glazed inside, and all the family without exception had to share in the stirring. I can remember that the only alcoholic enrichment of the pudding was either a half-pint or pint of porter from the pub around the corner at the end of Unicorn Street. As a little boy I went with a jug to fetch it with, I think, threeha'pence in my hand.

It used to be a matter of complete certainty in the family that mother's Christmas puddings were the best possible, and beyond rivalry. The puddings of friends around in the street were not comparable with hers; in fact not 'in the same street'. Theirs were too heavy, too solid, and too puddingy altogether. We were able to make comparisons in that way because there was a strange custom in the street of sending the children around to friends after Christmas dinner carrying samples of pudding for mutual assessment. This was a small example of the familiar and cosy atmosphere of a bygone Portsmouth street, where everybody knew everybody, rather as in a village.

That leads me to remember some of the names of families there before the century began, many of whose descendants are likely to be found still in other parts of the city. A Mrs Young, kept a little general shop where we children bought our farthing's worth of sweets, usually chocolate in penny slabs, divisible into four sections. Alternatively, chocolate cream was to be had, at the same price and similarly divisible.

Some of the family names seem more easily recalled than far more recent ones. Moxley, Calderwood, Hatch, Thomas, Shepherd, Cunningham, Lillywhite, Price, Gordon, Hamper and Ravenhill are a few of them. Charley Gordon, a son of one of them, had a wonderful and quite extraordinary wooden horse. It was not one of your ordinary toys, but one big enough to give a ride to the biggest of us, with saddle, stirrups and reins.

Those were the days when the memory of General Gordon of Khartoum was very fresh, and inevitably our Charles Gordon was General Gordon in those games. He had the name and the horse.

The tiny houses of Orange Street, Portsea, named after the royal Dutch House of Orange.

Marbles and Cherry Bobs

(First published 1 February 1967)

I think that my very earliest memory of all is my face close to some black material, with nearby a little line of black buttons. I can only think that I was in my mother's arms and that the black cloth and buttons were the Victorian dress which was almost uniform for women then. I couldn't have been more than a baby and Queen Victoria had still a dozen years to reign.

One more memory not quite so old might interest psychologists as an example of association of ideas. As a toddler I had gone to play in the street with the older boys, and had picked up from them in my innocence a swear word beginning with the letter B. I repeated this indoors, perhaps with some pride, within the hearing of my father. He promptly put me face down over his knees and smacked my rear. And here is the interesting point. Lying over his knees as he sat on a kitchen chair my view was nothing but the chair's wooden rungs. To this day, when I hear that swear word – a very common one – I see the wooden rungs of that chair. Scores of years have never rubbed out that connection.

Many children's games are recalled, hoops and marbles and conkers according to season. They scraped little circles in the gravel in the middle of the road, into which each player put an agreed number of marbles out of his precious stock in a little bag. The road was safe enough then; the only traffic was a horse-drawn cart or the milkman's trolley with its churn. Standing in the gutter, each youngster in turn had his chance of knocking out of the ring a marble, with his larger favourite 'taw'. It was remarkable how boys could lob one out of the ring at that distance.

As a variant, the game was played along a gutter, and every marble hit was the prize of the hitter. In cherry time the game was 'cherry bobs' up the spout. Two youngsters sitting on the pavement either side of a rainwater spout where it reached the ground would pop a cherry stone up with the flat of the hand. If on coming down again it struck another stone in the 'kitty' on the ground, that stone was the prize of the one shooting the stone up.

One game we played which if we had had more years or more sense we might not have done – not a regular game but a bit of mischief on only one occasion. Several older boys playing soldiers had made a rough sort of stretcher with two broomsticks and a bit of sacking. On this they placed me, the smallest of them, told me to shut my eyes and carried me to our front door. They fetched my mother and told her I was wounded. For a long moment my mother was taken in, and I think I can hear her now, wailing: 'Oh, it's only five minutes ago that I put his little jumper on!'

When I jumped up, alive and well, it was not surprising that she scolded the boys. The jumper, of course, was part of the sailor clothes that many boys and I wore at that time. By the way, the sailor cap was always a handy receptacle for conkers, marbles, etc., tucked in around the edge. The hatband was usually inscribed: HMS *Victory*.

There were other activities favoured by boys, which although not coming under the heading of games, were full of interest and good for training the hands in a sort of rough modelling. One was the making of hand warmers. Road excavations usually yielded an abundance of clay, and all the better if it happened to be the prized red Stamshaw clay.

The idea was to get a lump of the clay free of stones and, by banging and patting it, to make it into the shape of a perfect cube. This is not an easy job. Finally the inside of the cube was cut out with a penknife, leaving only the back, the sides and the bottom. Short bits of wire across the front made the hand-sized cube into a sort of fire grate. What the boys called touchwood was then used as fuel for the grate, and the job was supposed to be a hand-warmer in cold weather. Touchwood was merely scraps of dry rotting wood from anywhere like the underside of an old doorstep. The name possibly came from the old idea of firing the old muzzle-loading guns.

Boys long ago used to steal a ride behind horse-drawn vans, either on the tailboard should it be conveniently left horizontal, or just by hanging on anyhow. I think the fun of this was increased by the fact that other boys might yell the old cry: 'Whip behind, mister!' The driver would flick his long whip backwards and catch the hangers-on. I well remember going home once with a red weal across my cheek from such an adventure.

The memory of my mother's concern over my cut cheek brings me back home again to that little house which later years and different ideas were to condemn as not good enough. I was born in one such supposedly inadequate house, and have since had a number of homes, here and elsewhere, which were materially much finer, but none to me is more prized and precious as that 'home' of my early childhood.

Streets were quieter and safer in the old days as this evocative photograph of children at play in Cross Street, Portsea, shows.

School at the Ripe Old Age of Three

(First published 8 February 1967)

To return for a moment to that old house – there were two bedrooms above the front and back rooms, and from a small landing another flight led to a fairly spacious attic. Strange are the fancies and fears of childhood. Put to bed before my elders in one of the first-floor rooms, I was often quite sure that I heard footsteps come up to the landing outside the door, and then climb the further stairs to the attic. When I told of it I was always assured that nobody had come upstairs and that I was imagining it – but I was always quite sure of it.

Another childish memory of bedtime was connected with the old clock that stood on the mantelpiece of my bedroom. It had a wooden case with a glass front, and the lower part of the face showed a brass pendulum swinging rapidly to and fro. As I lay there staring unblinking at it, I thought that the pendulum, without stopping its swinging, moved steadily out at me, and then just before hitting my face it clicked back into the clock in a swift return.

I suppose I came near to being hypnotised by that old clock. The experts would know. I only know that those two bedtime memories have lasted all these years.

School? Yes, I went at the ripe old age of three to St John's Infant School at Bonfire Corner. I cannot remember any of the mechanics of learning to read, write or count. It seems to me I always could.

The name of our governess was Mrs Biggs, and I was very fond of her. Her husband was some official in the dockyard and they lived in King Street, where indeed a number of naval officers then lived.

About the only memories of the curriculum (apart from the Three Rs) that have remained with me are of needlework, knitting and some little poems we sung out in concert. The needlework consisted of hemming little rectangles of material along each side. The knitting was plain stitch, which I can still do with an effort. I don't remember graduating to purl stitch. The boys did this as well as the girls. I wonder how many Portsmouth boys who later joined the Navy found that simple teaching of use during 'make-and-mend' days? A great favourite poem was:

> Hang up the baby's stocking,
> Be sure you don't forget.
> The dear little dimpled darling
> Has never seen a Christmas yet.

The poems made no claim to a place among the immortals, but at least they introduced us to the pleasures of rhythm and rhyme.

Home and school indeed made our little lives, and the street was our safe playground. That street is still a clear picture to me now – from one end where the wall around Trinity Church with its overhanging trees looked down the length of the street, to the other end where we used to watch loads of faggots from the country being unloaded into the bakery, where old-fashioned ovens baked old-fashioned bread, mainly cottage loaves at tuppence a loaf.

Across the street from our house was a building we called the Sunday school. It was built on the ground where Wesley preached. The floor above it was an almshouse and occasionally we saw a couple of old women come out, but didn't quite understand what they were doing there.

Two pictures come back among others, of individuals who lived in street – quickly dissolving pictures like the bits one sees on television. One is of a young man striding along the pavement to his house. He was obviously what one might call 'merry', and was singing at the top of his voice an old music hall song of the time. The other picture is of a different sort. It is of a very stately and portly gentleman walking along, never seen except in top hat and frock coat. He had, I think, been a writer in the Navy and was now retired, and helped people with their money affairs, probably assisting with income tax problems. I see him now as one of the Victorian breed, soon to disappear in the coming of a very different world, in which the old stiff proprieties of dress and manner were to change greatly.

That brings me to two individuals of particular interest to this family. The story of any family would make interesting reading, not only to the family circle, but also often to others. Nearly a century ago my mother, then a girl of nineteen, was picking, not the roses of romance, but blackcurrants, in the garden of a whitewashed cottage by the very edge of the waters of Milford Haven in Pembrokeshire. The little place – less than a village – was, and is, called Hazelbeach. A young seaman, ashore from the Royal Navy ship HMS *Nankin* anchored nearby, looked over the garden wall. From there one's imagination must take over. That not unromantic meeting would have led to others, but who would want to peer more closely? It is enough to know that within months the two were married.

The old Orange Street chapel was made redundant with the building of a new place of worship in 1773. This building, remembered by Richard Esmond, was used as a school, and the upper galleries were converted to rooms for needy and elderly widows.

Make-and-mend day aboard a ship of Victoria's Navy when seamen could put their sewing skills to good use.

A Quiet Woman, but Plucky and Very Determined

(First published 15 February 1967)

That young woman was a rosy-cheeked girl, with (in her own words, years after) 'hair as black as a raven's wing'. That hair, parted in the centre, came down each side in natural waves, and did so until she died.

Her name was Mary Ann, which her daughters later, when they wanted to be affectionately cheeky, shortened or transformed into Polly. How I know not, or why. Her surname was decidedly Irish, which was unusual in that land of Evans, Jones, Jenkins and Williams. Long ago the Irish packet boats used to put in at Milford Haven. That may explain how the name was transplanted.

I was once told, when on my one visit to my mother's birthplace at Hazelbeach, that her grandfather, a stonemason, had built a chapel practically single-handed, inspired by John Wesley's evangelistic crusade. Farmer friends carried the stone for him. My rather amused thought on hearing this was that a Cork family

almost certainly of Catholic stock, had quickly succumbed to the Welsh Nonconformist atmosphere.

However, here was this young Irish-Welsh girl married to a blond young Sussex man from a very old Chichester family. His ship came back to Portsmouth. Here he rented for her a little house in Orange Street, and she, a girl who had never in her life been more than a mile or two from that cottage by the sea, was faced with a long frightening journey with a few-months-old baby in her arms. I would dearly like to know more about that lonely journey of hers, from the extreme southwest corner of Wales to a little street in Victorian Portsmouth. She crossed the Severn at some ferry up the river, for I have heard her speak of how kind and helpful the ferryman was to a young girl and baby stepping out alone into the unknown.

She broke her journey at Salisbury for one night, and must have been enormously relieved to reach the little house and her young husband and to settle down in the home where all her other children – five more of them – were to be born.

She was a quiet, rather retiring sort of woman always, but as that journey shows, she had the pluck and determination of the quiet sort with difficulties to be faced and to accomplish whatever had to be done.

She didn't see that cottage home by the sea for more than thirty years. There was no money for holidays and travelling. Eventually, when she had long been widowed, she went back with one of her sons for a little holiday and to see her aged father once more. It was her first and last return to the home of her youth.

It was not long after her arrival at Portsmouth that her young husband went on a three-year commission that lasted almost seven years. It included land service in the Ashanti War of 1874 as well as service afloat that was often concerned with chasing and capturing slave dhows off the African coast. His ships were of the period when Royal Navy vessels were still full-rigged but with an engine of sorts in reserve. My mother sometimes mentioned the names of two of them in later years – *Argus* and *Zebra*. The latter is the subject of one of those pictures worked in coloured wool on canvas, and shows – correctly of course – every rope and spar on the ship. This must have occupied many quiet hours of my father's time off watch at sea a century ago, and I still have it hanging on the wall. Its port side

shows nine gun ports, so it was probably an 18-gun frigate.

I have often studied that old picture, and indeed it speaks of those long months at sea with little or no distractions in the off-watch hours. In the picture the sea is divided abruptly into two areas, one light blue and the other very dark blue. Evidently his supply of one shade of blue had run out, and there was no chance at sea of renewing his supply.

I still wonder at the motives that induced young men of mid-Victorian times to change the ordinary life ashore for the tough life of the Royal Navy. My father had been an apprentice cabinet maker to his own father, and had thrown that up to go to sea. What was the attraction about 'salt junk' and 'hard tack', going aloft setting and reefing sails on swaying spars far above the sea or deck?

He was at one period 'captain of the foretop' on his ship. A landlubber can only guess just what that meant, especially in a storm. When he joined up, Nelson and Trafalgar were only fifty years away. Was it the romantic call of the sea, the hero worship, the wonder and attraction of tall ships and far-off places? Probably some or all of these.

He went soon after his marriage on that commission, the length of which would horrify present-day naval families, and my mother had no news of him for long stretches of time. Then there were no organisations concerning themselves with the welfare of naval families.

The picture of HMS Zebra *done in coloured wool by Richard Esmond's father while at sea.*

Brother Took up the Burden

(First published 22 February 1967)

People perforce stood upon their own two feet in the days when my father was at sea and carried on their lives without turning to any outside aid. A sailor's wife had her meagre half-pay from her absent husband, and didn't write letters complaining about its inadequacy, or about being separated from her husband.

And these were the conditions under which my mother made a real home for us all. Mother and family in that very modest but separate little house are to my mind just what amounted to that precious thing we call a home.

However humble, it was not merely a place, but an entity composed of close personal relationships. And 'separate' is the word, for I believe no conglomeration of sky-reaching flats can rival it or take its place. Beyond all, home was where 'Mum' was. A good definition of loss and emptiness would be when we children rushing in from school yelling 'Mum' found on extremely rare occasions no answer. And a feeling of peace and complete security when mother's answer came. Browning might have said for us: 'Mum's in her kitchen, all's right with the world.'

How it was done I don't know, but none of my mother's six children lacked food or clothing. All grew up to be useful citizens without a 'delinquent' among them.

We never thought ourselves badly off, and in fact had quite a good opinion of ourselves as a family. We had pennies where modern youngsters have pounds – and good luck to them. We were content in our modest sphere, and have come out of hard conditions better, perhaps, than was to be expected. I think that my father and mother would be proud to know that a number of their grandchildren and great-grandchildren are university graduates, some of them holding very responsible jobs.

But to get back to my father, and to the tragedy that hit the family when I was just five years old. He sailed the seven seas in peace and war for his twenty-one years of service in the old Navy of salt junk and hard tack; when it was better to put a hand into the sack of ship's biscuits in the dark, for then one wouldn't see the weevils. His last years of service were in the fine old troopers that used to run from Portsmouth to Bombay carrying troops to the India of Victoria. I can remember seeing them in the harbour – big white ships called *Jumna*, *Crocodile* and *Serapis*.

With his very modest pension then, my father retired from the Navy and got a job on a dockyard dredger. These vessels had saintly names – *St Dunstan* and *St Andrew* for instance. I remember getting into a boat at the Portsea pontoon with my mother and one or two of the younger members of the family, and my father rowing us out to see his ship – the *St Andrew*. It came on to rain heavily as soon as we started and my father pulled into shelter under the viaduct. It must have been high tide, for once there he stood up in the boat and held on to the girders to keep the boat steady. That frightened my mother, and I can still hear her begging him to be careful. On board the dredger I remember vaguely the iron deck and the great frightening hole in the centre of the ship with the water at the bottom where the iron buckets went down to the seabed.

It could not have been very long after that visit that a boat from that dredger – perhaps the same boat – took men from the ship with a cable to tie up to a buoy out in the middle of the harbour. Two men, one of them my father, climbed out of the boat and on to the buoy to attach the cable. The buoy tipped and threw them into the sea. From the few details I learned later in life, both were wearing sea-boots and oilskins. Perhaps it was a foul day for August, for that was the month, and 1892 was the year – a lifetime ago.

One of the two was rescued at once, but not my father. The men did all they could, but those who know the harbour understand that when making or ebbing the tide can run up to six or seven knots. I have heard of an oar being thrown from the boat for him to grasp, which instead struck his head. These are bits of talk that I gathered many years after, for a child of five knew little of it all. He was not seen again until his body was picked up days later and brought ashore by an Eastney fisherman near No Man's Land Fort at Spithead.

So a man who had spent his life on the wide oceans came home to lose it in the narrow waters almost in sight of his own doorstep, still a comparatively young man. I have heard that my mother was prostrate with grief on hearing the news. Later – it may have been the next day – the captain of the dredger came to see her. For some reason she took me into the room to stand at her knee while he spoke. I remember clearly how he told her they had searched long before giving up. I understood dimly what it was all about, but don't think the full meaning really registered on the child of five that I was.

At that time my eldest brother was a boy of fourteen. He had left school and had secured a job on the bookstall at the old East Southsea Station at

Granada Road. He told me many years later how a male friend of the family had come to the book-stall and said: 'Bill, you are to come home – your father's drowned.'Just like that!

At a mature age he was still wondering at the man's lack of delicacy in delivering such a message in such a heartless way. That brother of mine, at fourteen, had to become the man of the family. I have never ceased to admire the way he carried the heavy burden on his young shoulders for the next dozen years. He took the responsibility for the three youngest members of the family with all seriousness and never a complaint. He became, I realise now, older than his years, with no time for the usual pursuits of youth.

Of all the men I have known, there has been none I honour more. He saw to it that we younger ones had better chances than fate had meted out to him, yet I realised in after years that he had natural abilities that never had a chance to blossom.

A last memory before I finish. My mother often took me on Sunday afternoons to visit the grave in Kingston Cemetery, where just over the railings in St Mary's Road the big beds of wallflowers broad-cast their lovely perfume.

The huge white troopship HMS Jumna *was a familiar sight at Portsmouth. She was one of five used to transport troops and their families to India; her sister ships were* Serapis, Crocodile, Euphrates *and* Malabar.